AF483584

Mr. Fascination and the Fascination Machines

Written and Illustrated *by* Michael Jasorka

Story adapted from

'Fascination: A lifetime Boardwalk Adventure'

By Randy Senna, *Editor*

READ GUIDE:

1
2
Left to Right
Top to Bottom
3
4
5

SINCE BEFORE YOU WERE BORN
ORIGIN OF THE MACHINES

SINCE BEFORE YOU WERE BORN
WELCOME TO ONE OF THE LAST, OLD TIME BOARDWALK GAMES!..
FASCINATION!..
1920's TO CHICAGO WORLDS FAIR
WHERE YOU PAY FOR THE FUN AND THE PRIZE IS JUST A BONUS!..
HERE AT TRIBUTES AND TRADITIONS, WE PLAY THE SAME FASCINATION TABLES THAT WERE AT OLYMPIC PARK IN IT'S FINAL YEARS OF THE 1960'S!.. OF COURSE, A GREAT GAME WOULD HAVE A LONG HISTORIC PAST!..
- ALRIGHT.. FIVE LIGHTS IN A ROW IN ANY DIRECTION, WILL GET YOUR WINNER - TOP TO BOTTOM, SIDE TO SIDE, OR CORNER TO CORNER!.. AND AT THE SOUND OF THE BELL, WE'LL DO JUST THAT!..
- READY?..
Mr. Fascination

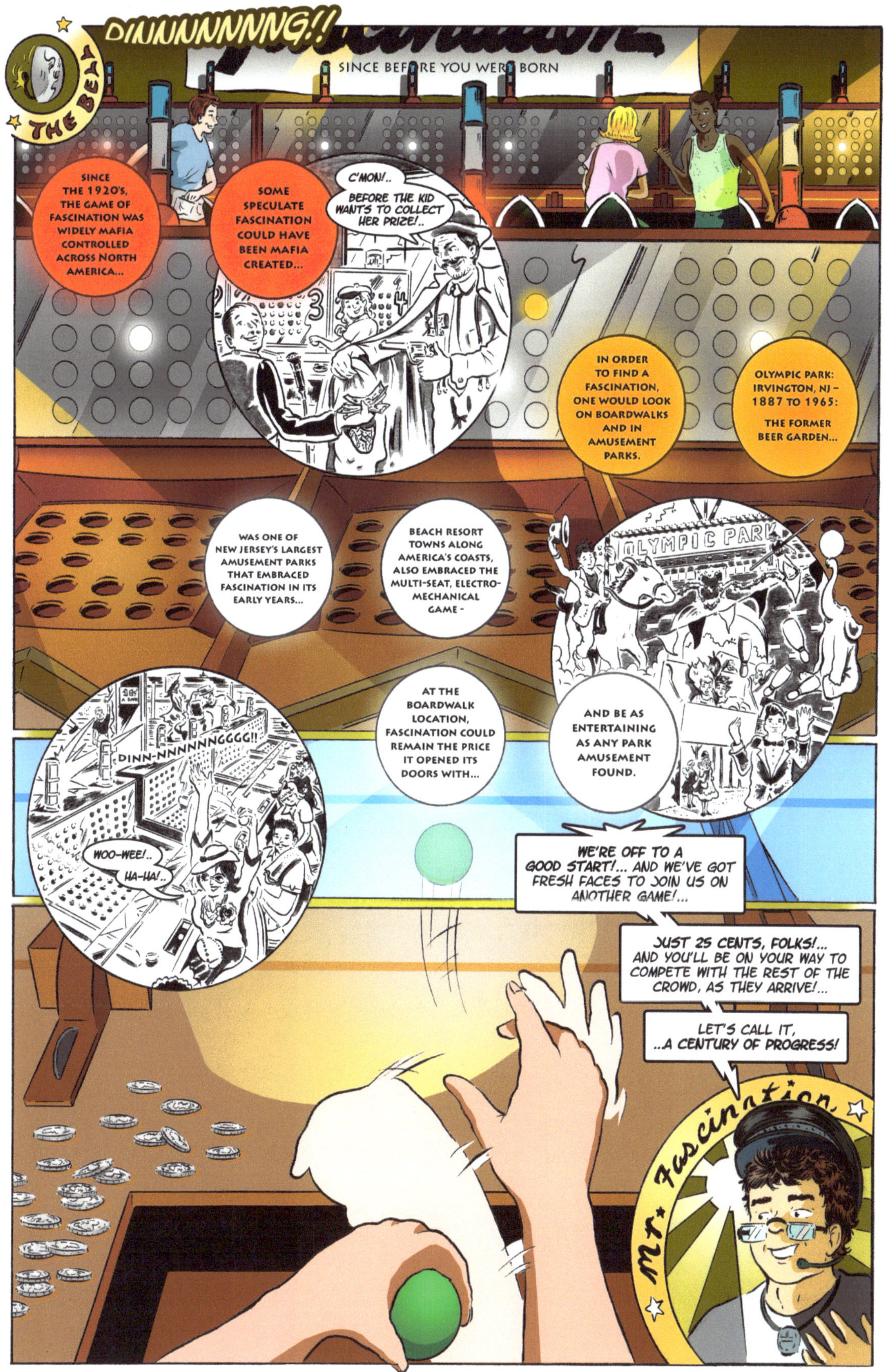

DINNNNNNG!!
THE BEV
SINCE BEFORE YOU WERE BORN
SINCE THE 1920'S, THE GAME OF FASCINATION WAS WIDELY MAFIA CONTROLLED ACROSS NORTH AMERICA...
SOME SPECULATE FASCINATION COULD HAVE BEEN MAFIA CREATED...
C'MON!.. BEFORE THE KID WANTS TO COLLECT HER PRIZE!..
IN ORDER TO FIND A FASCINATION, ONE WOULD LOOK ON BOARDWALKS AND IN AMUSEMENT PARKS.
OLYMPIC PARK: IRVINGTON, NJ – 1887 TO 1965: THE FORMER BEER GARDEN...
WAS ONE OF NEW JERSEY'S LARGEST AMUSEMENT PARKS THAT EMBRACED FASCINATION IN ITS EARLY YEARS...
BEACH RESORT TOWNS ALONG AMERICA'S COASTS, ALSO EMBRACED THE MULTI-SEAT, ELECTRO-MECHANICAL GAME -
OLYMPIC PARK
AT THE BOARDWALK LOCATION, FASCINATION COULD REMAIN THE PRICE IT OPENED ITS DOORS WITH...
AND BE AS ENTERTAINING AS ANY PARK AMUSEMENT FOUND.
DINN-NNNNNGGGG!!
WOO-WEE!.. HA-HA!..
WE'RE OFF TO A GOOD START!... AND WE'VE GOT FRESH FACES TO JOIN US ON ANOTHER GAME!...
JUST 25 CENTS, FOLKS!... AND YOU'LL BE ON YOUR WAY TO COMPETE WITH THE REST OF THE CROWD, AS THEY ARRIVE!...
LET'S CALL IT, ..A CENTURY OF PROGRESS!
MR. Fascination

SINCE BEFORE YOU WERE BORN

A CENTURY OF PROGRESS:

THE 1933 CHICAGO WORLD'S FAIR.

THE SLOGAN CAME OUT OF THE FAIR'S DEBUT EXHIBITION OF THE LATEST ADVANCES IN SOCIAL SCIENCES, TECHNOLOGY AND BEYOND.

FITTING ALL THREE: THE GAME OF FASCINATION... THE ELECTRONIC COMBINATION OF SKI BALL AND BINGO.

WITH A PATENT HELD BY JOHN TAYLOR GIBBS OF UTAH, GIBBS TOOK FASCINATION TO THE 1933 CHICAGO WORLD'S FAIR...

SOON, IMITATORS WOULD APPEAR, BUT ONLY TO BE SWEPT UNDER GAMBLING LAWS SET AROUND BOARDWALK AMUSEMENTS...

INSTEAD OF HAVING FASCINATION'S BLANK CIRCLE MATRIX, GAMES LIKE POKERINO AND BINGORINO...

USED PLAYING CARD SUITS OR BINGO LETTERS AS A MATRIX... ALLOWING A PLAYER TO MAKE BETS ON THE SCORES.

IT'S HIS BET!..

AS THE IMITATORS FELL, THE SIMPLE RACE TO LIGHT-UP A BINGO LINE HAD A DIFFERENT FATE...

IN 1947, FASCINATION WAS DEEMED A "GAME OF SKILL" BY THE NEW YORK SUPREME COURT.

EVEN AFTER OUT-LIVING GAMBLING PROHIBITION, FASCINATION FACED THE OBSTACLE OF AN EXISTENCE IN AMUSEMENT PARKS...

AS THE PARKS THAT HOUSED THE FASCINATION GAME EVENTUALLY DEVELOPED A PAY ONCE ADMISSION -

GIVING LITTLE OR NO INTEREST TO PAY FOR A GAME OF FASCINATION AFTER PAYING ENTRY FOR THE PARK.

ON THE BEACH BOARDWALKS, WHERE THERE WAS NO ENTRY FEE, IT WAS ANOTHER STORY - THE FLAME WAS LIT...

BUT IT NEEDED AN EVEN BIGGER FLAME IN ORDER TO SURVIVE.

DINNNNNN-NNNNG!

- YOU FOLKS WALKING IN!.. GET READY FOR THE NEXT WIN!.. AND WE'LL ONCE AGAIN, BEGIN AT THE SOUND OF THE BELL! --

..WE HAVE ONE LEFT TO LIGHT-UP TWO RED STOP LIGHTS!.. AND ONE, WITH ONLY THREE STOP LIGHTS LEFT ON THE GOLD LINE!.. WHO WILL IT BE??..

Mr. Fascinat

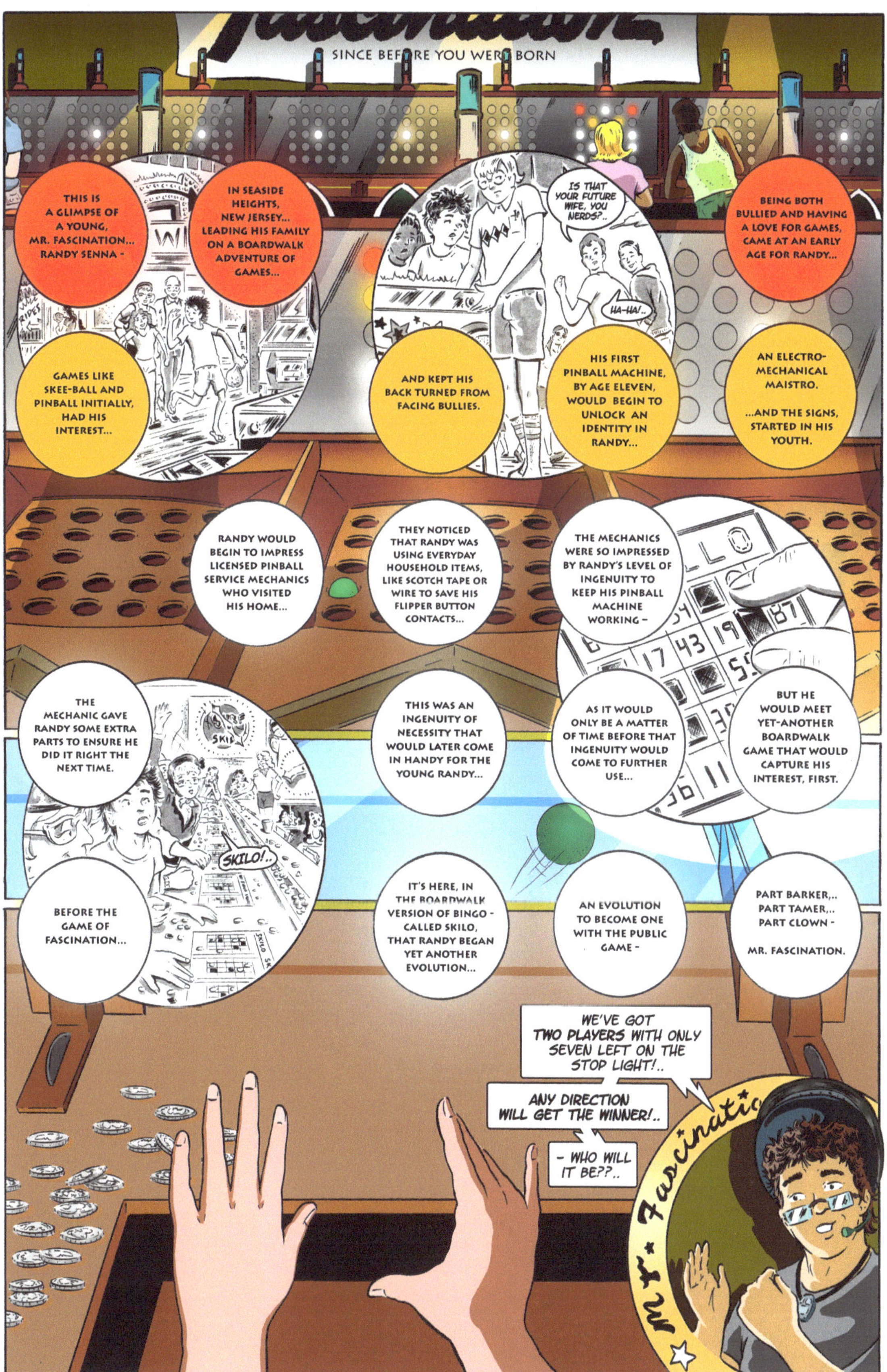

FASCINATION
SINCE BEFORE YOU WERE BORN

THIS IS A GLIMPSE OF A YOUNG, MR. FASCINATION... RANDY SENNA -

IN SEASIDE HEIGHTS, NEW JERSEY... LEADING HIS FAMILY ON A BOARDWALK ADVENTURE OF GAMES...

IS THAT YOUR FUTURE WIFE, YOU NERDS?..

HA-HA!..

BEING BOTH BULLIED AND HAVING A LOVE FOR GAMES, CAME AT AN EARLY AGE FOR RANDY...

GAMES LIKE SKEE-BALL AND PINBALL INITIALLY, HAD HIS INTEREST...

AND KEPT HIS BACK TURNED FROM FACING BULLIES.

HIS FIRST PINBALL MACHINE, BY AGE ELEVEN, WOULD BEGIN TO UNLOCK AN IDENTITY IN RANDY...

AN ELECTRO-MECHANICAL MAISTRO.

...AND THE SIGNS, STARTED IN HIS YOUTH.

RANDY WOULD BEGIN TO IMPRESS LICENSED PINBALL SERVICE MECHANICS WHO VISITED HIS HOME...

THEY NOTICED THAT RANDY WAS USING EVERYDAY HOUSEHOLD ITEMS, LIKE SCOTCH TAPE OR WIRE TO SAVE HIS FLIPPER BUTTON CONTACTS...

THE MECHANICS WERE SO IMPRESSED BY RANDY'S LEVEL OF INGENUITY TO KEEP HIS PINBALL MACHINE WORKING -

THE MECHANIC GAVE RANDY SOME EXTRA PARTS TO ENSURE HE DID IT RIGHT THE NEXT TIME.

THIS WAS AN INGENUITY OF NECESSITY THAT WOULD LATER COME IN HANDY FOR THE YOUNG RANDY...

AS IT WOULD ONLY BE A MATTER OF TIME BEFORE THAT INGENUITY WOULD COME TO FURTHER USE...

BUT HE WOULD MEET YET-ANOTHER BOARDWALK GAME THAT WOULD CAPTURE HIS INTEREST, FIRST.

SKILO!..

BEFORE THE GAME OF FASCINATION...

IT'S HERE, IN THE BOARDWALK VERSION OF BINGO - CALLED SKILO, THAT RANDY BEGAN YET ANOTHER EVOLUTION...

AN EVOLUTION TO BECOME ONE WITH THE PUBLIC GAME -

PART BARKER,... PART TAMER,... PART CLOWN - MR. FASCINATION.

WE'VE GOT TWO PLAYERS WITH ONLY SEVEN LEFT ON THE STOP LIGHT!..

ANY DIRECTION WILL GET THE WINNER!..

- WHO WILL IT BE??..

MR. Fascination

THE BEAT
DINNNNNNNG!!
SINCE BEFORE YOU WERE BORN
YEAH, BABE!.. WE DID IT!!
AN OBSESSION BEGINS
- AND WE HAVE A WINNER ON THE GOLD LINE!..
THE YOUNG LADY WITH THE PINK SHIRT!..
IT'S AS IF THE PRINCESS HAS LEFT HER COURT - BUT NOT WITHOUT HER KNIGHT!!..
ALLL-RIGHT, WE'RE GONNA DO IT AGAIN...
- AT THE BELL.. ROLL EM UP - LIGHT EM' UP, AND WIN!..
Mr. Fascinat

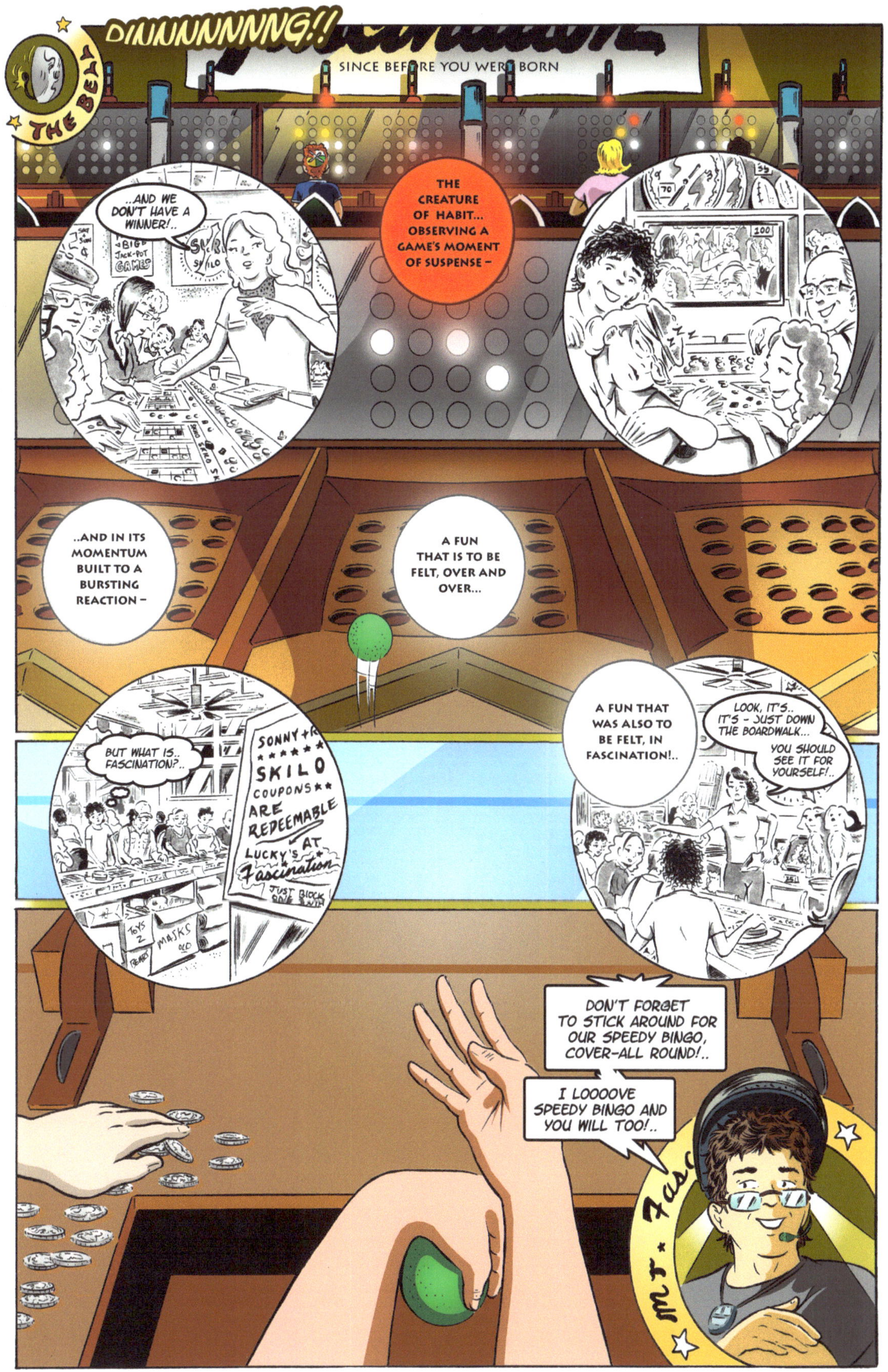

DINNNNNNNG!!
SINCE BEFORE YOU WERE BORN
THE BELL
..AND WE DON'T HAVE A WINNER!..
BIG JACK-POT GAMES
SKILO
THE CREATURE OF HABIT... OBSERVING A GAME'S MOMENT OF SUSPENSE –
100
70
..AND IN ITS MOMENTUM BUILT TO A BURSTING REACTION –
A FUN THAT IS TO BE FELT, OVER AND OVER...
BUT WHAT IS.. FASCINATION?..
SONNY + R
SKILO COUPONS ARE REDEEMABLE AT Fascination
JUST BLOCK ONE
TOYS 2 MASKS
A FUN THAT WAS ALSO TO BE FELT, IN FASCINATION!..
LOOK, IT'S.. IT'S – JUST DOWN THE BOARDWALK... YOU SHOULD SEE IT FOR YOURSELF!..
DON'T FORGET TO STICK AROUND FOR OUR SPEEDY BINGO, COVER-ALL ROUND!..
I LOOOOVE SPEEDY BINGO AND YOU WILL TOO!..
Mr. Fasc

FASCINATION
SINCE BEFORE YOU WERE BORN
FUNTOWN U.S.A.
I THOUGHT I HAD SEEN EVERYTHING THERE WAS TO SEE -
AND BEEN IN EVERY PLACE THERE WAS TO BE!..
SHADOWED BY SMALL STANDS AND GAMES OF CHANCE, THE YOUNG RANDY, MOVED IN...
FASCINATION
DINNNNN-NNNNG!
LUCKY'S
TOWELS
Just 5¢ AND WIN!
PASSING THE TOWEL STAND, THE CIGARETTE STAND AND THE CANDY STAND, TO FINALLY REVEALING ITS PEARL...
RELUCTANTLY, HE ENTERED... AS A FEELING OF BEING OUT OF PLACE HITS HIM -
MAYBE... I SHOULD JUST... GO THE CARNIVAL ARCADE OR SOMETHING?..
THOUGH IT WAS A SIMILAR CROWD TO SKILO...
THIS WASN'T SKILO THAT THEY WERE PLAYING...
HAHA
QUIT
BE BRAVE... BE BRAVE...
WELL - C'MON IN!..
HAVE A SEAT... RELAX YOUR FEET -
WE'RE JUST ABOUT TO START A NEW GAME OF FASCINATION!..
mr. Fascinati

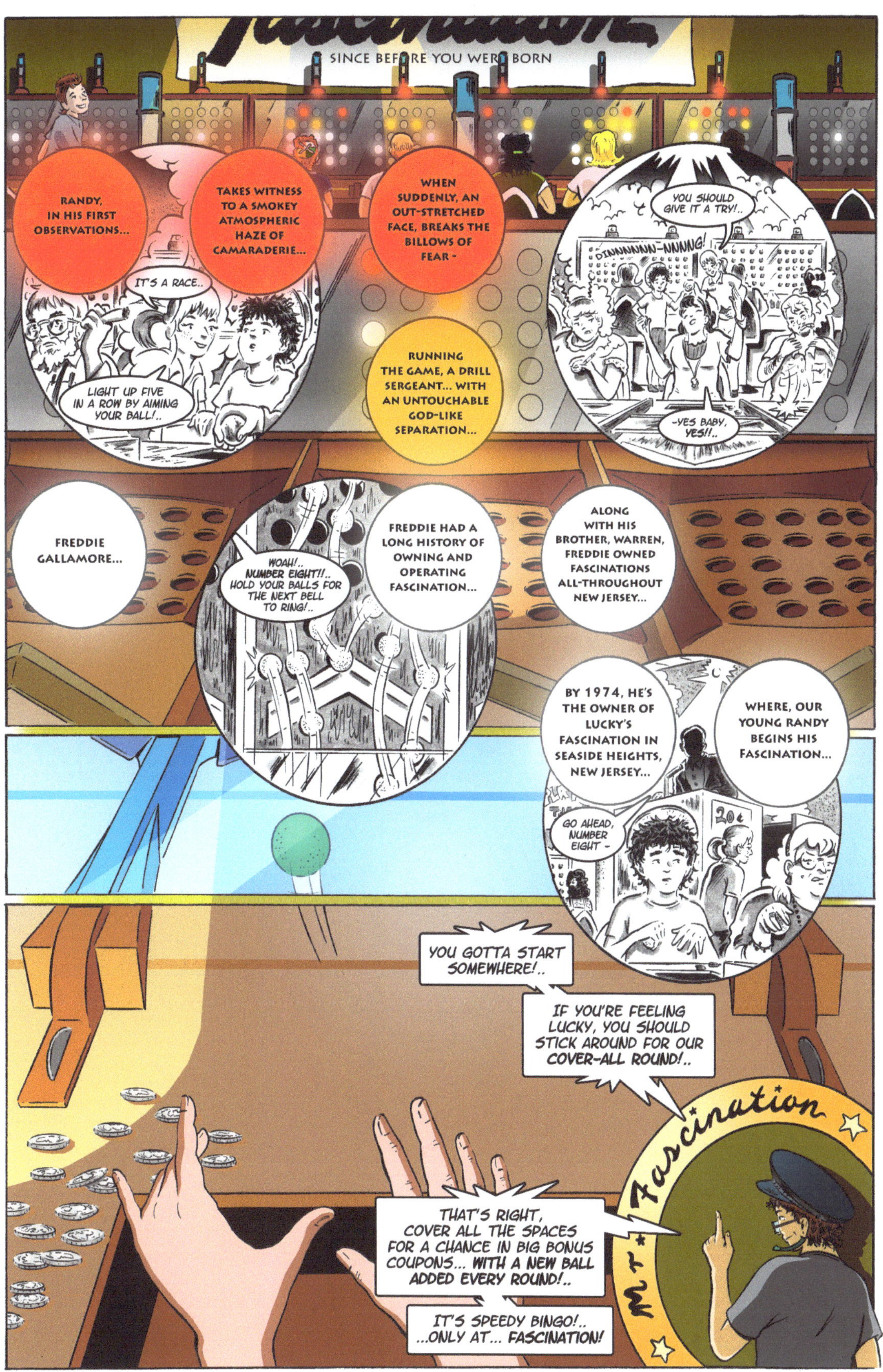

SINCE BEFORE YOU WERE BORN
RANDY, IN HIS FIRST OBSERVATIONS...
TAKES WITNESS TO A SMOKEY ATMOSPHERIC HAZE OF CAMARADERIE...
WHEN SUDDENLY, AN OUT-STRETCHED FACE, BREAKS THE BILLOWS OF FEAR -
IT'S A RACE..
LIGHT UP FIVE IN A ROW BY AIMING YOUR BALL!..
RUNNING THE GAME, A DRILL SERGEANT... WITH AN UNTOUCHABLE GOD-LIKE SEPARATION...
YOU SHOULD GIVE IT A TRY!..
DINNNNN-NNNNG!
-YES BABY, YES!!..
FREDDIE GALLAMORE...
WOAH!.. NUMBER EIGHT!!.. HOLD YOUR BALLS FOR THE NEXT BELL TO RING!..
FREDDIE HAD A LONG HISTORY OF OWNING AND OPERATING FASCINATION...
ALONG WITH HIS BROTHER, WARREN, FREDDIE OWNED FASCINATIONS ALL-THROUGHOUT NEW JERSEY...
BY 1974, HE'S THE OWNER OF LUCKY'S FASCINATION IN SEASIDE HEIGHTS, NEW JERSEY...
WHERE, OUR YOUNG RANDY BEGINS HIS FASCINATION...
GO AHEAD, NUMBER EIGHT -
20¢
YOU GOTTA START SOMEWHERE!..
IF YOU'RE FEELING LUCKY, YOU SHOULD STICK AROUND FOR OUR COVER-ALL ROUND!..
Mr. Fascination
THAT'S RIGHT, COVER ALL THE SPACES FOR A CHANCE IN BIG BONUS COUPONS... WITH A NEW BALL ADDED EVERY ROUND!..
IT'S SPEEDY BINGO!.. ...ONLY AT... FASCINATION!

9

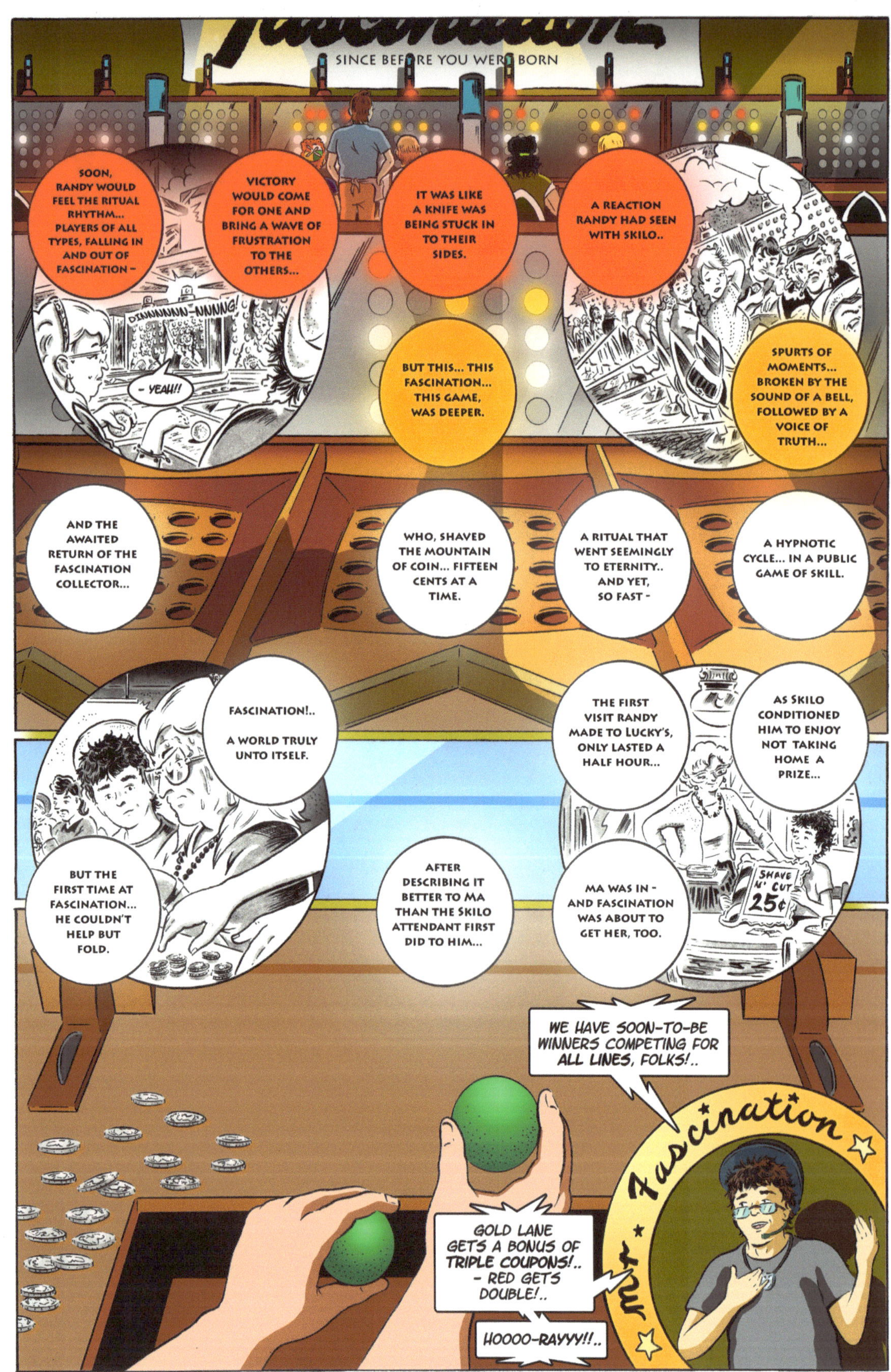
FASCINATION
SINCE BEFORE YOU WERE BORN

SOON, RANDY WOULD FEEL THE RITUAL RHYTHM... PLAYERS OF ALL TYPES, FALLING IN AND OUT OF FASCINATION –

DINNNNNN-NNNNG!

– YEAH!!

VICTORY WOULD COME FOR ONE AND BRING A WAVE OF FRUSTRATION TO THE OTHERS...

IT WAS LIKE A KNIFE WAS BEING STUCK IN TO THEIR SIDES.

A REACTION RANDY HAD SEEN WITH SKILO..

BUT THIS... THIS FASCINATION... THIS GAME, WAS DEEPER.

SPURTS OF MOMENTS... BROKEN BY THE SOUND OF A BELL, FOLLOWED BY A VOICE OF TRUTH...

AND THE AWAITED RETURN OF THE FASCINATION COLLECTOR...

WHO, SHAVED THE MOUNTAIN OF COIN... FIFTEEN CENTS AT A TIME.

A RITUAL THAT WENT SEEMINGLY TO ETERNITY.. AND YET, SO FAST –

A HYPNOTIC CYCLE... IN A PUBLIC GAME OF SKILL.

FASCINATION!.. A WORLD TRULY UNTO ITSELF.

THE FIRST VISIT RANDY MADE TO LUCKY'S, ONLY LASTED A HALF HOUR...

AS SKILO CONDITIONED HIM TO ENJOY NOT TAKING HOME A PRIZE...

BUT THE FIRST TIME AT FASCINATION... HE COULDN'T HELP BUT FOLD.

AFTER DESCRIBING IT BETTER TO MA THAN THE SKILO ATTENDANT FIRST DID TO HIM...

MA WAS IN – AND FASCINATION WAS ABOUT TO GET HER, TOO.

SHAVE N' CUT 25¢

WE HAVE SOON-TO-BE WINNERS COMPETING FOR ALL LINES, FOLKS!..

GOLD LANE GETS A BONUS OF TRIPLE COUPONS!.. – RED GETS DOUBLE!..

HOOOO-RAYYY!!..

mr. Fascination

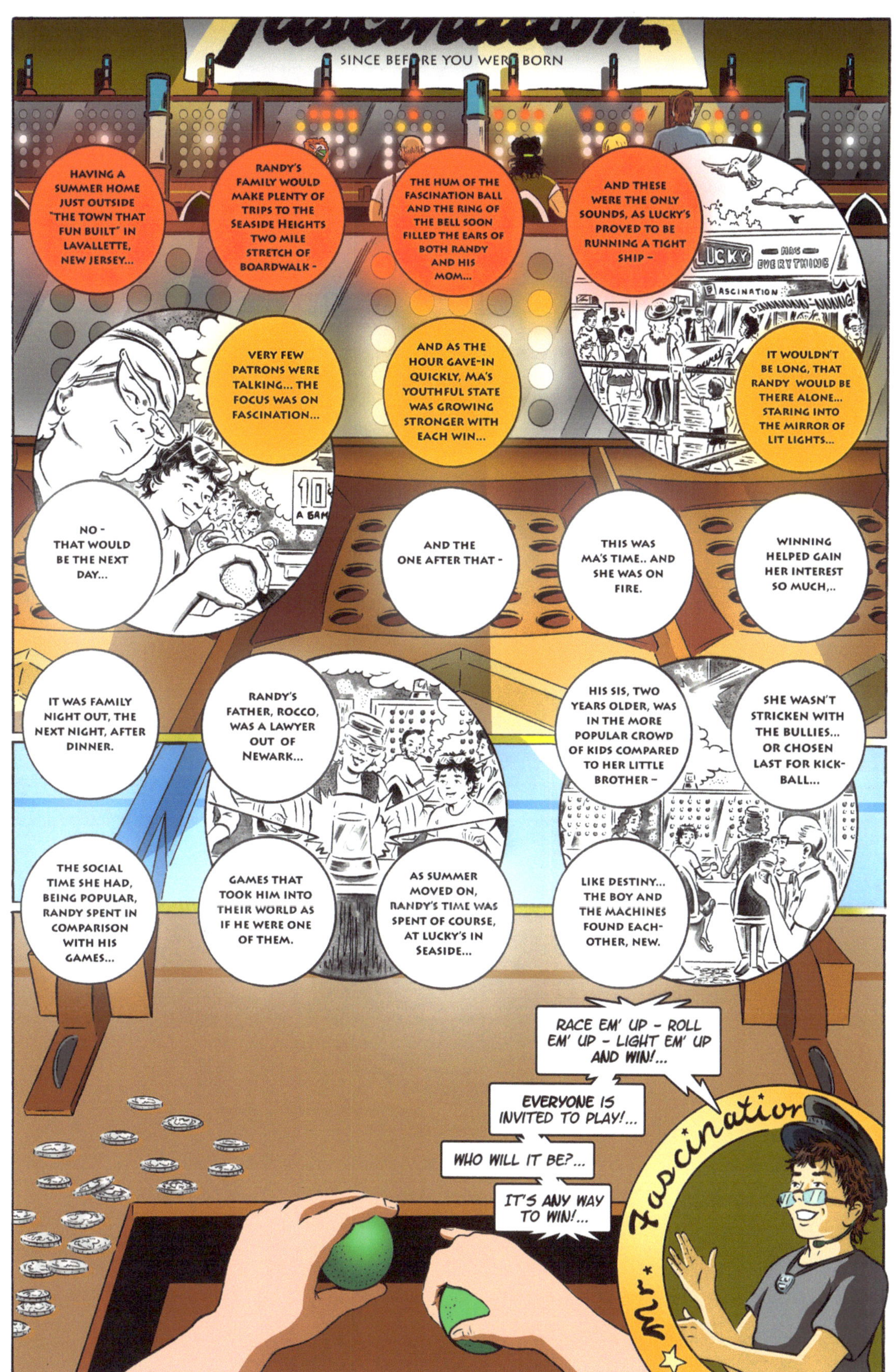

fascination
SINCE BEFORE YOU WERE BORN

HAVING A SUMMER HOME JUST OUTSIDE "THE TOWN THAT FUN BUILT" IN LAVALLETTE, NEW JERSEY...

RANDY'S FAMILY WOULD MAKE PLENTY OF TRIPS TO THE SEASIDE HEIGHTS TWO MILE STRETCH OF BOARDWALK -

THE HUM OF THE FASCINATION BALL AND THE RING OF THE BELL SOON FILLED THE EARS OF BOTH RANDY AND HIS MOM...

AND THESE WERE THE ONLY SOUNDS, AS LUCKY'S PROVED TO BE RUNNING A TIGHT SHIP -

LUCKY — HAS — EVERYTHING
FASCINATION

VERY FEW PATRONS WERE TALKING... THE FOCUS WAS ON FASCINATION...

AND AS THE HOUR GAVE-IN QUICKLY, MA'S YOUTHFUL STATE WAS GROWING STRONGER WITH EACH WIN...

IT WOULDN'T BE LONG, THAT RANDY WOULD BE THERE ALONE... STARING INTO THE MIRROR OF LIT LIGHTS...

NO - THAT WOULD BE THE NEXT DAY...

AND THE ONE AFTER THAT -

THIS WAS MA'S TIME.. AND SHE WAS ON FIRE.

WINNING HELPED GAIN HER INTEREST SO MUCH,..

IT WAS FAMILY NIGHT OUT, THE NEXT NIGHT, AFTER DINNER.

RANDY'S FATHER, ROCCO, WAS A LAWYER OUT OF NEWARK...

HIS SIS, TWO YEARS OLDER, WAS IN THE MORE POPULAR CROWD OF KIDS COMPARED TO HER LITTLE BROTHER –

SHE WASN'T STRICKEN WITH THE BULLIES... OR CHOSEN LAST FOR KICK-BALL...

THE SOCIAL TIME SHE HAD, BEING POPULAR, RANDY SPENT IN COMPARISON WITH HIS GAMES...

GAMES THAT TOOK HIM INTO THEIR WORLD AS IF HE WERE ONE OF THEM.

AS SUMMER MOVED ON, RANDY'S TIME WAS SPENT OF COURSE, AT LUCKY'S IN SEASIDE...

LIKE DESTINY... THE BOY AND THE MACHINES FOUND EACH-OTHER, NEW.

RACE EM' UP - ROLL EM' UP - LIGHT EM' UP AND WIN!...

EVERYONE IS INVITED TO PLAY!...

WHO WILL IT BE?...

IT'S ANY WAY TO WIN!...

Mr. Fascination

DINNNNNNNG!!
THE BELT
ONCE BEFORE YOU WERE BORN
- YEAH, I WON!..
ALRIGHT!
THE OBSESSION CONTINUES
WE HAVE... A WINNER!.. CONGRATULATIONS ON GETTING THE DIAGONAL LINE!.. WITH FIVE LEFT ON THE STOP-LIGHT -
NEARLY A PERFECT GAME!..
ALRIGHT, WE'RE GOING TO MAKE THIS NEXT RACE, A SPECIAL RACE...
WE'RE GONNA MAKE IT A FREE PLAY GIVE-AWAY...
WHOEVER WINS THIS GAME, GETS THE COUPONS AND A FREE GAME ON THE TABLE!..
THAT'LL LET YOU PLAY ALL THE GAMES FREE UNTIL THE NEXT COVER-ALL.. JUST FOR WINNING THIS GAME - ANY LINE YOU WIN ON!..
..READY?
Mr. Fascina

DINNNNNNG!!
THE BEAT
SINCE BEFORE YOU WERE BORN
RANDY'S PLAYING TOOK TO AN OBSESSION...
BEGINNING WITH NOT GETTING OUT OF THE CHAIR TO EAT... OR GOING TO THE BATHROOM –
RANDY STAYED DEDICATED TO HIS TABLE #1 FOR TWELVE HOUR DAYS, THE ENTIRE SUMMER...
Lucky's
REGULARS BEGAN TO HATE HIM, AS HE WOULD ALWAYS BE THERE... MANY WOULD NOT EVEN DARE PLAY –
ELDERLY WOMEN WOULD SEND THEIR HUSBANDS TO HECKLE HIM IN ORDER TO WIN..
YOU'RE SUPPOSE TO BE SMOKING THEM, RANDY!... NOT THE OTHER WAY AROUND!.. HA-HA!..

Fascination
SINCE BEFORE YOU WERE BORN
STAFF ONLY
THE SMOKE IS FROM THE HEAT YOU'RE CAUSIN', KID!..
NOW RANDY, THE FUTURE MR. FASCINATION, WAS OPEN TO FRIENDSHIP –
..ESPECIALLY WITH THOSE WHO RAN HIS BELOVED FASCINATION...
BUT BEING CLOSE TO THE OPERATOR'S BOOTH, STARTED TO BECOME A HANDI-CAP...
A FRIENDSHIP WAS RIGHT THERE FOR THEM TO HAVE.. BUT INSTEAD, THEY PICKED ON HIM.
SO, RANDY PICKED UP HIS COUPONS AND MOVED TO THE FARTHEST TABLE FROM THE CONTROL BOOTH –
TABLE 23 WOULD BE HIS FAVORITE AFTER #1... AND HE WOULD LATER FIND FAVORITES IN OTHERS...
BUT THAT CAME OUT OF RANDY DISCOVERING THAT EACH TABLE HAD IT'S OWN PERSONALITY...
NOT BECAUSE LUCKY'S OPERATORS DECIDED TO LIMIT RANDY'S WINNING.
Still 15¢
WHICH, THEY DID – THEY HAD TO... AS RANDY WAS BECOMING TOO GOOD AT FASCINATION.
AND WE HAVE.. FIVE WITH EIGHT STOP LIGHTS TO GO!..
IT'S ANYONE'S GAME!.. ANYONE!.. COULD BE THE WINNER!..
Mr. Fascina

14

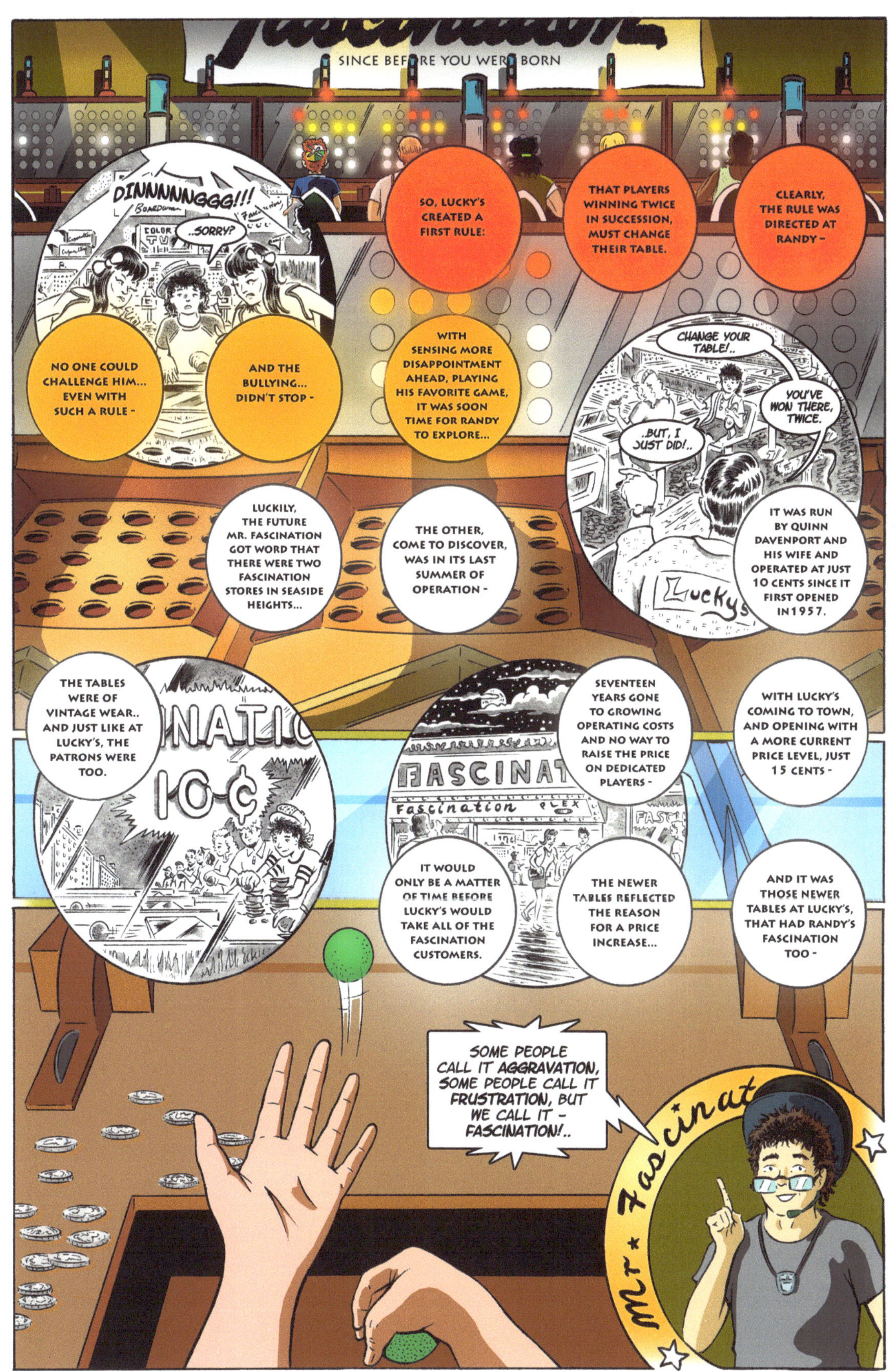

FASCINATION
SINCE BEFORE YOU WERE BORN
DINNNNNGGG!!!
..SORRY?
COLOR TV
NO ONE COULD CHALLENGE HIM... EVEN WITH SUCH A RULE -
AND THE BULLYING... DIDN'T STOP -
SO, LUCKY'S CREATED A FIRST RULE:
WITH SENSING MORE DISAPPOINTMENT AHEAD, PLAYING HIS FAVORITE GAME, IT WAS SOON TIME FOR RANDY TO EXPLORE...
THAT PLAYERS WINNING TWICE IN SUCCESSION, MUST CHANGE THEIR TABLE.
CLEARLY, THE RULE WAS DIRECTED AT RANDY -
CHANGE YOUR TABLE!..
YOU'VE WON THERE, TWICE.
..BUT, I JUST DID!..
Lucky's
LUCKILY, THE FUTURE MR. FASCINATION GOT WORD THAT THERE WERE TWO FASCINATION STORES IN SEASIDE HEIGHTS...
THE OTHER, COME TO DISCOVER, WAS IN ITS LAST SUMMER OF OPERATION -
IT WAS RUN BY QUINN DAVENPORT AND HIS WIFE AND OPERATED AT JUST 10 CENTS SINCE IT FIRST OPENED IN 1957.
THE TABLES WERE OF VINTAGE WEAR.. AND JUST LIKE AT LUCKY'S, THE PATRONS WERE TOO.
NATIO 10¢
FASCINAT
Fascination
SEVENTEEN YEARS GONE TO GROWING OPERATING COSTS AND NO WAY TO RAISE THE PRICE ON DEDICATED PLAYERS -
WITH LUCKY'S COMING TO TOWN, AND OPENING WITH A MORE CURRENT PRICE LEVEL, JUST 15 CENTS -
IT WOULD ONLY BE A MATTER OF TIME BEFORE LUCKY'S WOULD TAKE ALL OF THE FASCINATION CUSTOMERS.
THE NEWER TABLES REFLECTED THE REASON FOR A PRICE INCREASE...
AND IT WAS THOSE NEWER TABLES AT LUCKY'S, THAT HAD RANDY'S FASCINATION TOO -
SOME PEOPLE CALL IT AGGRAVATION, SOME PEOPLE CALL IT FRUSTRATION, BUT WE CALL IT - FASCINATION!..
Mr. Fascinat

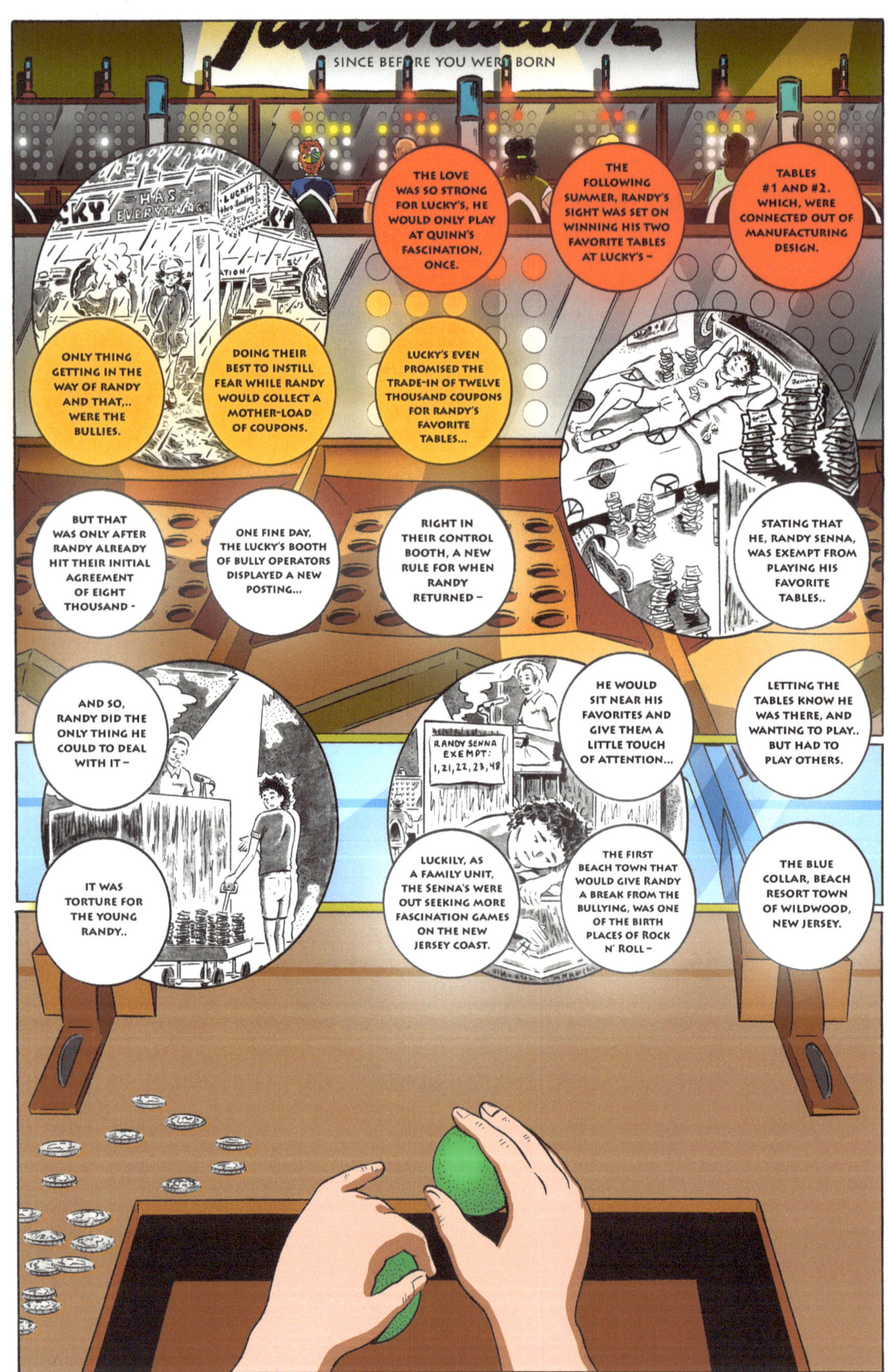
SINCE BEFORE YOU WERE BORN
LUCKY'S "HAS EVERYTHING!"
THE LOVE WAS SO STRONG FOR LUCKY'S, HE WOULD ONLY PLAY AT QUINN'S FASCINATION, ONCE.
THE FOLLOWING SUMMER, RANDY'S SIGHT WAS SET ON WINNING HIS TWO FAVORITE TABLES AT LUCKY'S –
TABLES #1 AND #2. WHICH, WERE CONNECTED OUT OF MANUFACTURING DESIGN.
ONLY THING GETTING IN THE WAY OF RANDY AND THAT,.. WERE THE BULLIES.
DOING THEIR BEST TO INSTILL FEAR WHILE RANDY WOULD COLLECT A MOTHER-LOAD OF COUPONS.
LUCKY'S EVEN PROMISED THE TRADE-IN OF TWELVE THOUSAND COUPONS FOR RANDY'S FAVORITE TABLES...
STATING THAT HE, RANDY SENNA, WAS EXEMPT FROM PLAYING HIS FAVORITE TABLES..
BUT THAT WAS ONLY AFTER RANDY ALREADY HIT THEIR INITIAL AGREEMENT OF EIGHT THOUSAND –
ONE FINE DAY, THE LUCKY'S BOOTH OF BULLY OPERATORS DISPLAYED A NEW POSTING...
RIGHT IN THEIR CONTROL BOOTH, A NEW RULE FOR WHEN RANDY RETURNED –
AND SO, RANDY DID THE ONLY THING HE COULD TO DEAL WITH IT –
RANDY SENNA EXEMPT: 1, 21, 22, 23, 48
HE WOULD SIT NEAR HIS FAVORITES AND GIVE THEM A LITTLE TOUCH OF ATTENTION...
LETTING THE TABLES KNOW HE WAS THERE, AND WANTING TO PLAY.. BUT HAD TO PLAY OTHERS.
IT WAS TORTURE FOR THE YOUNG RANDY..
LUCKILY, AS A FAMILY UNIT, THE SENNA'S WERE OUT SEEKING MORE FASCINATION GAMES ON THE NEW JERSEY COAST.
THE FIRST BEACH TOWN THAT WOULD GIVE RANDY A BREAK FROM THE BULLYING, WAS ONE OF THE BIRTH PLACES OF ROCK N' ROLL –
THE BLUE COLLAR, BEACH RESORT TOWN OF WILDWOOD, NEW JERSEY.

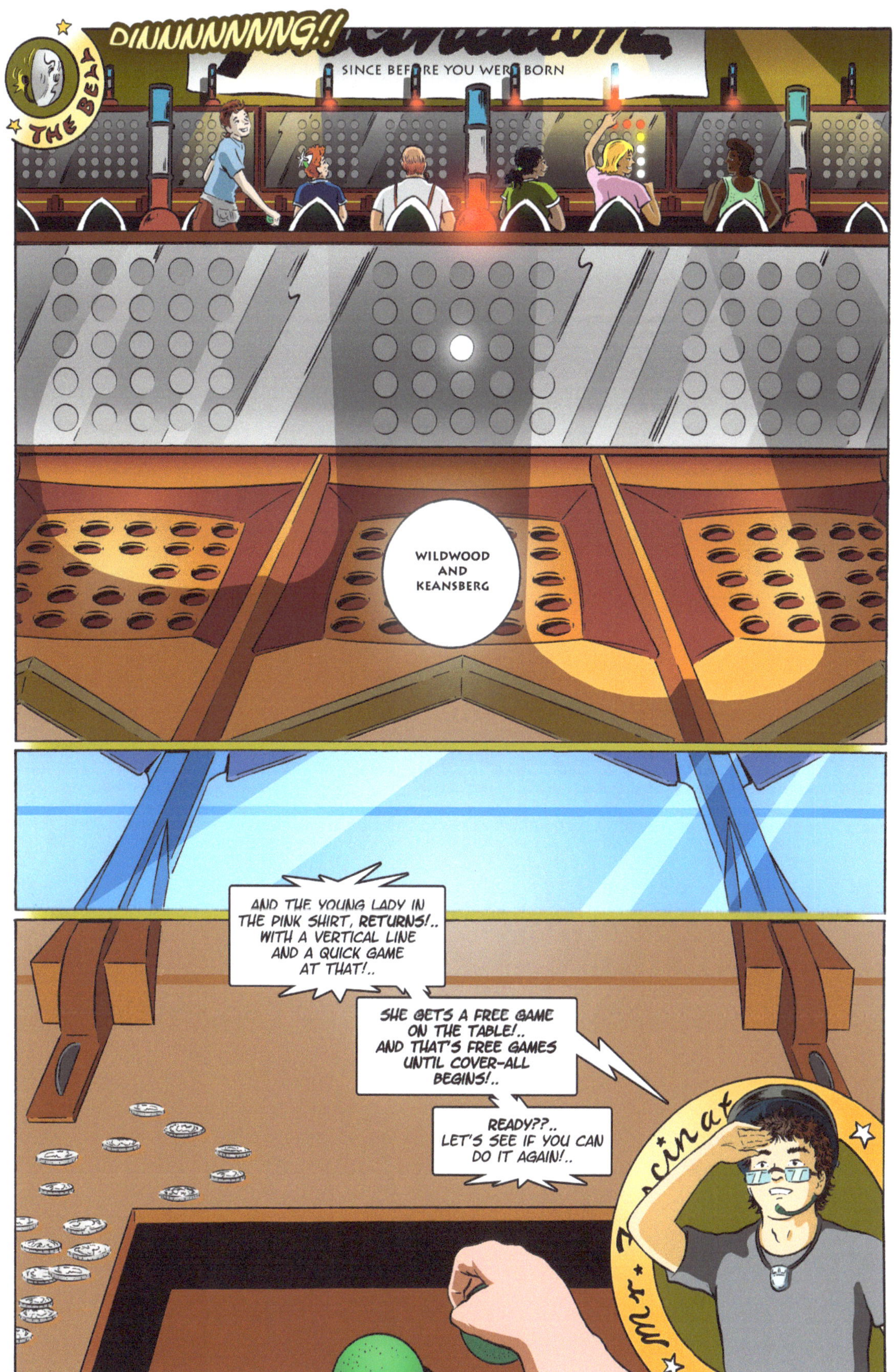
DINNNNNNNG!!
THE BEAT
SINCE BEFORE YOU WERE BORN
WILDWOOD AND KEANSBERG
AND THE YOUNG LADY IN THE PINK SHIRT, RETURNS!.. WITH A VERTICAL LINE AND A QUICK GAME AT THAT!..
SHE GETS A FREE GAME ON THE TABLE!.. AND THAT'S FREE GAMES UNTIL COVER-ALL BEGINS!..
READY??.. LET'S SEE IF YOU CAN DO IT AGAIN!..

DINNNNNNG!!
THE BELL
SINCE BEFORE YOU WERE BORN
ALONG WITH THE JOY OF PLAYING FASCINATION WITH HIS FAMILY –
THE TIME AWAY FROM SEASIDE, WAS A HEALTHY ONE FOR THE FUTURE MR. FASCINATION...
Winner EVERY GAME
FASCIN
AND IT ALLOWED FOR RANDY TO MAKE OBSERVATIONS OF HOW PLAYERS PLAYED FASCINATION ELSEWHERE –
HOUSE OF LIGHTS
OLYMPIC WILDWOOD, NJ
AND MORE IMPORTANTLY, HOW THE OWNERS OPERATED IT.
ALRIGHTY.. HERE WE GO, FOLKS!..
WELCOME TO OLYMPIC FASCINATION, HOUSE OF LIGHTS!..

FASCINATION
SINCE BEFORE YOU WERE BORN
WILDWOOD BACK THEN, WAS A WILD PLACE..
RANDY AND FAMILY WOULD PLAY IN CONTINUOUS PACKED HOUSES OF FASCINATION..
AND LIKE A WELL-OILED MACHINE, OLYMPIC FASCINATION RAN UNDER THE PLEASANT COMMAND OF MARTY SHAPIRO...
MARTY WOULD USE A CREW OF TEENAGE BOY COIN COLLECTORS...
WHO, WOULD BE RUNNING IN AND OUT - FROM BEHIND THE TABLES, COLLECTING COINS AT WARP SPEED.
MARTY WAS PARTNERS WITH WARREN GALLAMORE, THE BROTHER OF THE SEASIDE LUCKY'S FASCINATION OWNER, FREDDIE GALLAMORE –
BOTH OF THEM BROUGHT THE OLYMPIC MACHINES TO WILDWOOD IN 1968... AFTER OLYMPIC PARK CLOSED.
THEREFORE CALLING IT, "OLYMPIC ENTERPRISES FASCINATION."
WITH MARTY FILLING THE BUSINESS SIDE OF FASCINATION, AND WARREN FILLING THE ELECTRICAL-MECHANICAL ENGINEER SIDE –
RANDY, THE FUTURE MR. FASCINATION, WAS ABLE TO OBSERVE BOTH MEN AS MENTORS WHEN VISITING WILDWOOD...
NO WASTED TIME.. RIGHT, MARTY?!..
CONTINUOUSLY RESEARCHING THEIR FASCINATION... LIFESTYLE.
OLYMPIC PARK
SMILE
HOUSE OF LIGHTS

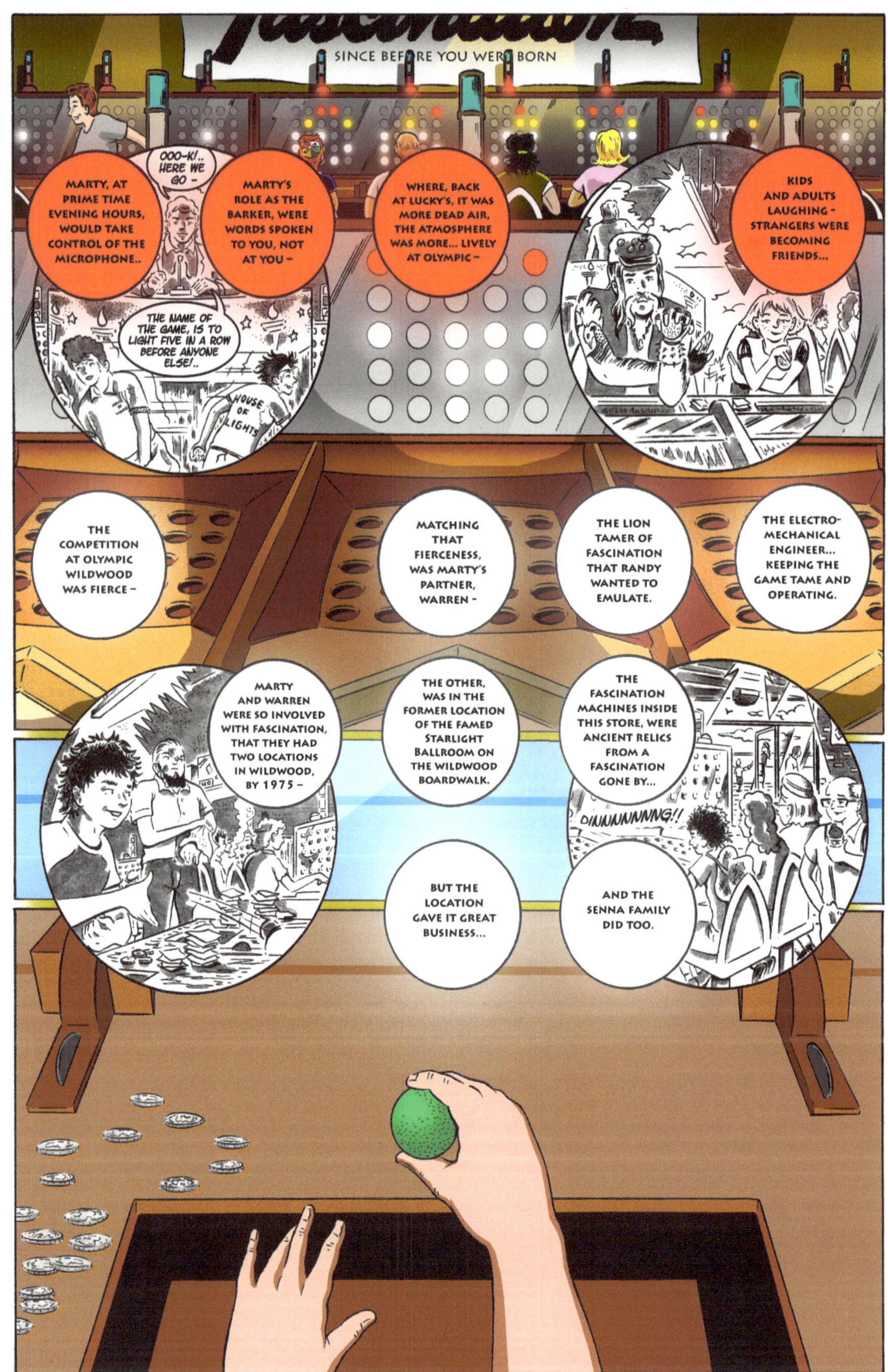
fascination
SINCE BEFORE YOU WERE BORN
MARTY, AT PRIME TIME EVENING HOURS, WOULD TAKE CONTROL OF THE MICROPHONE..
OOO-K!.. HERE WE GO -
MARTY'S ROLE AS THE BARKER, WERE WORDS SPOKEN TO YOU, NOT AT YOU -
THE NAME OF THE GAME, IS TO LIGHT FIVE IN A ROW BEFORE ANYONE ELSE!..
HOUSE OF LIGHTS
WHERE, BACK AT LUCKY'S, IT WAS MORE DEAD AIR, THE ATMOSPHERE WAS MORE... LIVELY AT OLYMPIC -
KIDS AND ADULTS LAUGHING - STRANGERS WERE BECOMING FRIENDS...
THE COMPETITION AT OLYMPIC WILDWOOD WAS FIERCE -
MATCHING THAT FIERCENESS, WAS MARTY'S PARTNER, WARREN -
THE LION TAMER OF FASCINATION THAT RANDY WANTED TO EMULATE.
THE ELECTRO-MECHANICAL ENGINEER... KEEPING THE GAME TAME AND OPERATING.
MARTY AND WARREN WERE SO INVOLVED WITH FASCINATION, THAT THEY HAD TWO LOCATIONS IN WILDWOOD, BY 1975 -
THE OTHER, WAS IN THE FORMER LOCATION OF THE FAMED STARLIGHT BALLROOM ON THE WILDWOOD BOARDWALK.
THE FASCINATION MACHINES INSIDE THIS STORE, WERE ANCIENT RELICS FROM A FASCINATION GONE BY...
DINNNNNNNG!!
BUT THE LOCATION GAVE IT GREAT BUSINESS...
AND THE SENNA FAMILY DID TOO.

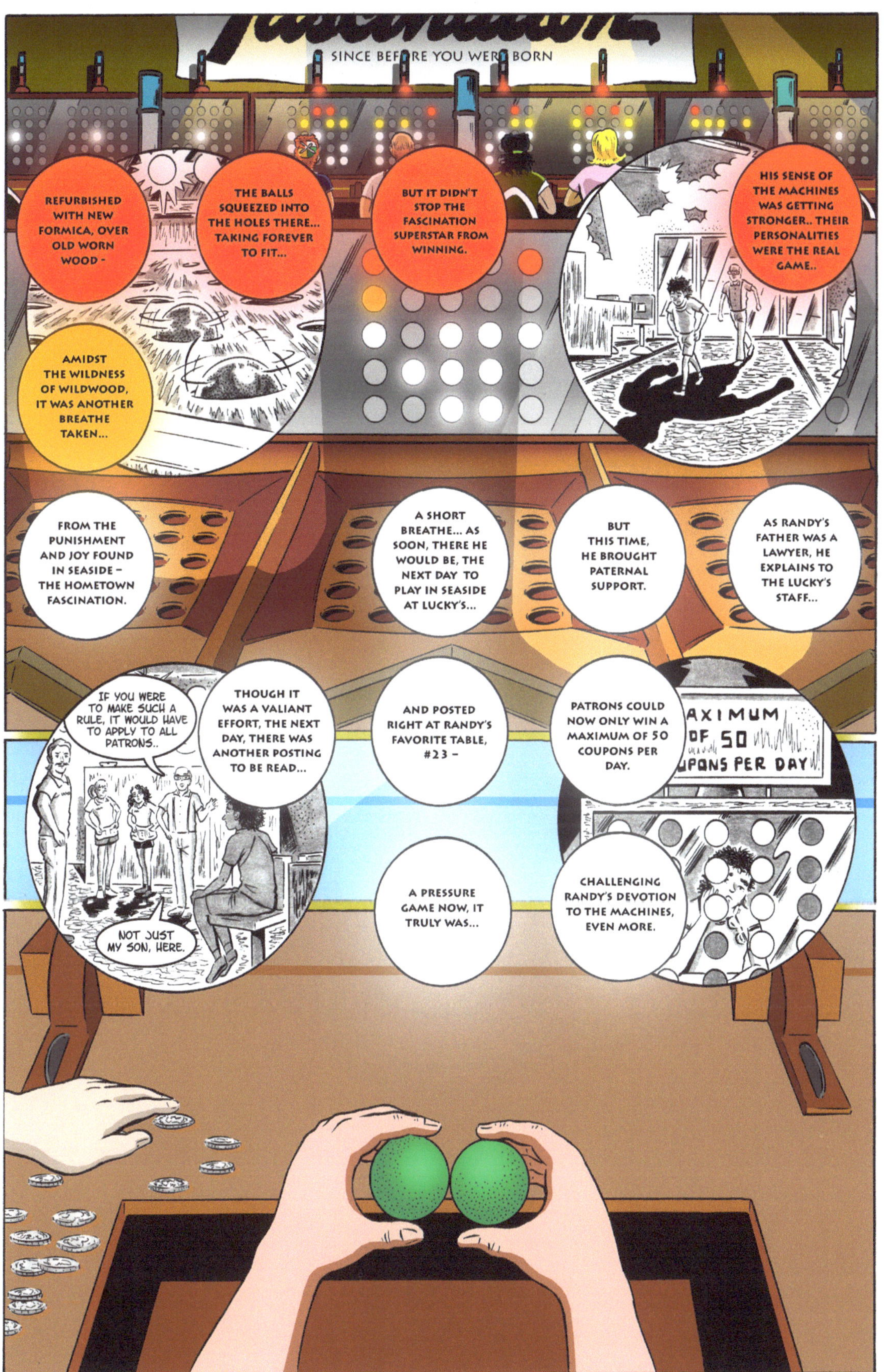
fascination
SINCE BEFORE YOU WERE BORN
REFURBISHED WITH NEW FORMICA, OVER OLD WORN WOOD -
THE BALLS SQUEEZED INTO THE HOLES THERE... TAKING FOREVER TO FIT...
BUT IT DIDN'T STOP THE FASCINATION SUPERSTAR FROM WINNING.
HIS SENSE OF THE MACHINES WAS GETTING STRONGER.. THEIR PERSONALITIES WERE THE REAL GAME..
AMIDST THE WILDNESS OF WILDWOOD, IT WAS ANOTHER BREATHE TAKEN...
FROM THE PUNISHMENT AND JOY FOUND IN SEASIDE – THE HOMETOWN FASCINATION.
A SHORT BREATHE... AS SOON, THERE HE WOULD BE, THE NEXT DAY TO PLAY IN SEASIDE AT LUCKY'S...
BUT THIS TIME, HE BROUGHT PATERNAL SUPPORT.
AS RANDY'S FATHER WAS A LAWYER, HE EXPLAINS TO THE LUCKY'S STAFF...
IF YOU WERE TO MAKE SUCH A RULE, IT WOULD HAVE TO APPLY TO ALL PATRONS..
THOUGH IT WAS A VALIANT EFFORT, THE NEXT DAY, THERE WAS ANOTHER POSTING TO BE READ...
AND POSTED RIGHT AT RANDY'S FAVORITE TABLE, #23 –
PATRONS COULD NOW ONLY WIN A MAXIMUM OF 50 COUPONS PER DAY.
MAXIMUM OF 50 COUPONS PER DAY
NOT JUST MY SON, HERE.
A PRESSURE GAME NOW, IT TRULY WAS...
CHALLENGING RANDY'S DEVOTION TO THE MACHINES, EVEN MORE.

21

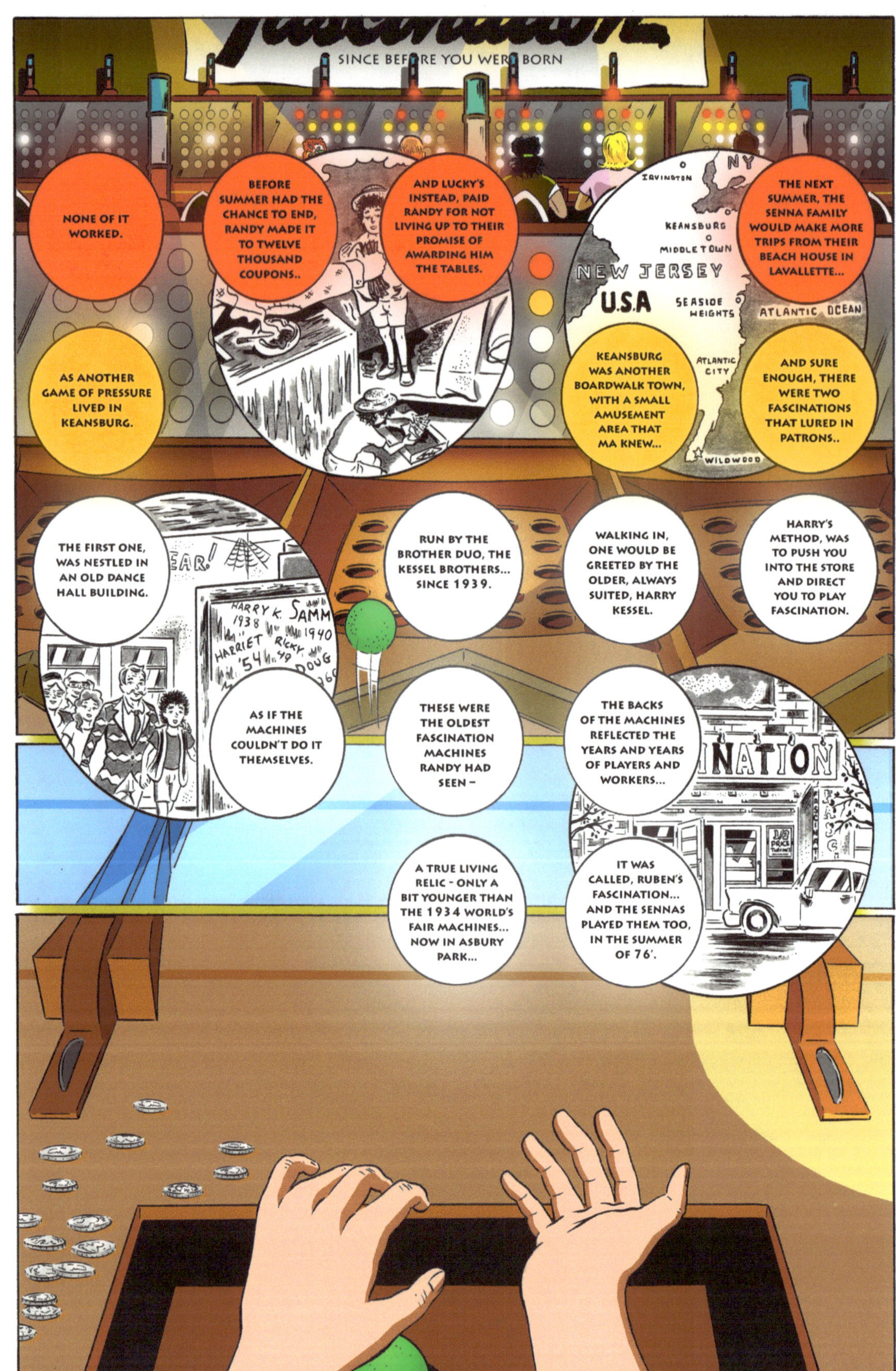

fascination
SINCE BEFORE YOU WERE BORN

NONE OF IT WORKED.

BEFORE SUMMER HAD THE CHANCE TO END, RANDY MADE IT TO TWELVE THOUSAND COUPONS..

AND LUCKY'S INSTEAD, PAID RANDY FOR NOT LIVING UP TO THEIR PROMISE OF AWARDING HIM THE TABLES.

THE NEXT SUMMER, THE SENNA FAMILY WOULD MAKE MORE TRIPS FROM THEIR BEACH HOUSE IN LAVALLETTE...

AS ANOTHER GAME OF PRESSURE LIVED IN KEANSBURG.

KEANSBURG WAS ANOTHER BOARDWALK TOWN, WITH A SMALL AMUSEMENT AREA THAT MA KNEW...

AND SURE ENOUGH, THERE WERE TWO FASCINATIONS THAT LURED IN PATRONS..

NY
IRVINGTON
KEANSBURG
MIDDLETOWN
NEW JERSEY
U.S.A
SEASIDE HEIGHTS
ATLANTIC OCEAN
ATLANTIC CITY
WILDWOOD

THE FIRST ONE, WAS NESTLED IN AN OLD DANCE HALL BUILDING.

EAR!
HARRY K. SAMM
1938
1940
HARRIET
RICKY
'54
'49
DOUG

RUN BY THE BROTHER DUO, THE KESSEL BROTHERS... SINCE 1939.

WALKING IN, ONE WOULD BE GREETED BY THE OLDER, ALWAYS SUITED, HARRY KESSEL.

HARRY'S METHOD, WAS TO PUSH YOU INTO THE STORE AND DIRECT YOU TO PLAY FASCINATION.

AS IF THE MACHINES COULDN'T DO IT THEMSELVES.

THESE WERE THE OLDEST FASCINATION MACHINES RANDY HAD SEEN –

THE BACKS OF THE MACHINES REFLECTED THE YEARS AND YEARS OF PLAYERS AND WORKERS...

INATION
1/2 PRICE

A TRUE LIVING RELIC - ONLY A BIT YOUNGER THAN THE 1934 WORLD'S FAIR MACHINES... NOW IN ASBURY PARK...

IT WAS CALLED, RUBEN'S FASCINATION... AND THE SENNAS PLAYED THEM TOO, IN THE SUMMER OF 76'.

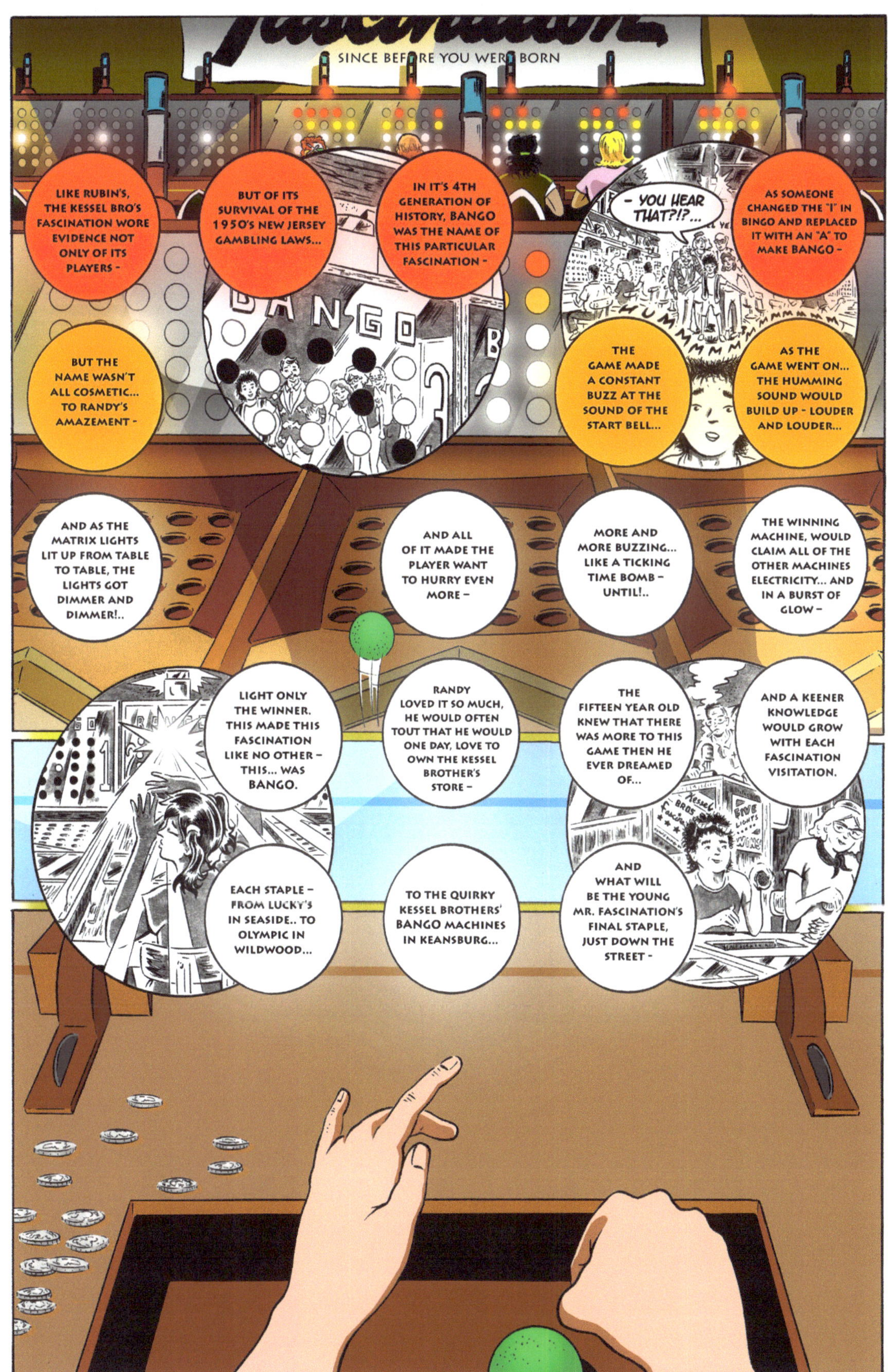
Fascination
SINCE BEFORE YOU WERE BORN
LIKE RUBIN'S, THE KESSEL BRO'S FASCINATION WORE EVIDENCE NOT ONLY OF ITS PLAYERS –
BUT OF ITS SURVIVAL OF THE 1950'S NEW JERSEY GAMBLING LAWS...
IN IT'S 4TH GENERATION OF HISTORY, BANGO WAS THE NAME OF THIS PARTICULAR FASCINATION –
– YOU HEAR THAT?!?...
AS SOMEONE CHANGED THE "I" IN BINGO AND REPLACED IT WITH AN "A" TO MAKE BANGO –
BUT THE NAME WASN'T ALL COSMETIC... TO RANDY'S AMAZEMENT –
THE GAME MADE A CONSTANT BUZZ AT THE SOUND OF THE START BELL...
AS THE GAME WENT ON... THE HUMMING SOUND WOULD BUILD UP - LOUDER AND LOUDER...
AND AS THE MATRIX LIGHTS LIT UP FROM TABLE TO TABLE, THE LIGHTS GOT DIMMER AND DIMMER!..
AND ALL OF IT MADE THE PLAYER WANT TO HURRY EVEN MORE –
MORE AND MORE BUZZING... LIKE A TICKING TIME BOMB – UNTIL!..
THE WINNING MACHINE, WOULD CLAIM ALL OF THE OTHER MACHINES ELECTRICITY... AND IN A BURST OF GLOW –
LIGHT ONLY THE WINNER. THIS MADE THIS FASCINATION LIKE NO OTHER – THIS... WAS BANGO.
RANDY LOVED IT SO MUCH, HE WOULD OFTEN TOUT THAT HE WOULD ONE DAY, LOVE TO OWN THE KESSEL BROTHER'S STORE –
THE FIFTEEN YEAR OLD KNEW THAT THERE WAS MORE TO THIS GAME THEN HE EVER DREAMED OF...
AND A KEENER KNOWLEDGE WOULD GROW WITH EACH FASCINATION VISITATION.
EACH STAPLE – FROM LUCKY'S IN SEASIDE.. TO OLYMPIC IN WILDWOOD...
TO THE QUIRKY KESSEL BROTHERS' BANGO MACHINES IN KEANSBURG...
AND WHAT WILL BE THE YOUNG MR. FASCINATION'S FINAL STAPLE, JUST DOWN THE STREET –

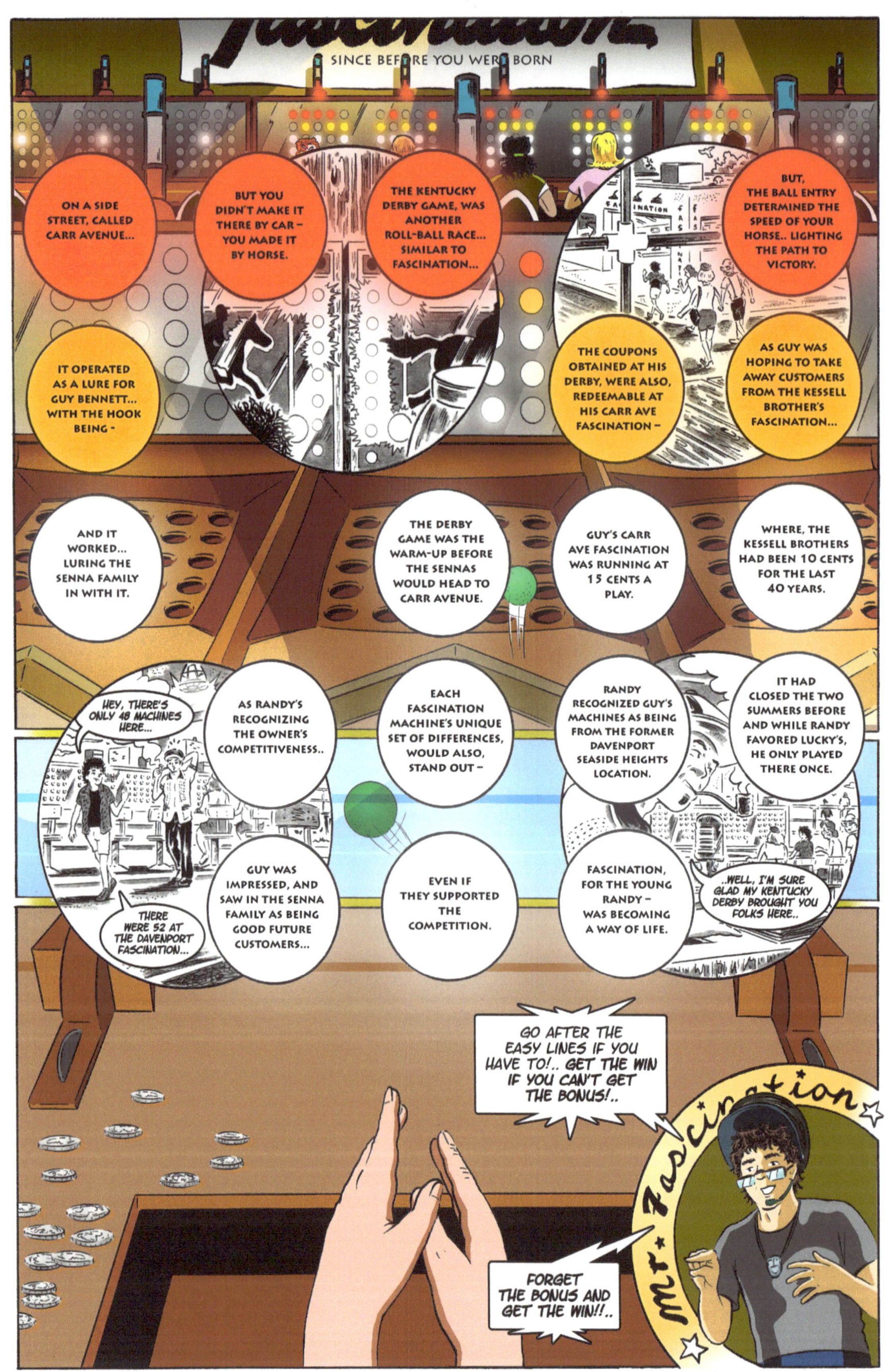
SINCE BEFORE YOU WERE BORN

ON A SIDE STREET, CALLED CARR AVENUE...

BUT YOU DIDN'T MAKE IT THERE BY CAR – YOU MADE IT BY HORSE.

THE KENTUCKY DERBY GAME, WAS ANOTHER ROLL-BALL RACE... SIMILAR TO FASCINATION...

BUT, THE BALL ENTRY DETERMINED THE SPEED OF YOUR HORSE.. LIGHTING THE PATH TO VICTORY.

IT OPERATED AS A LURE FOR GUY BENNETT... WITH THE HOOK BEING –

THE COUPONS OBTAINED AT HIS DERBY, WERE ALSO, REDEEMABLE AT HIS CARR AVE FASCINATION –

AS GUY WAS HOPING TO TAKE AWAY CUSTOMERS FROM THE KESSELL BROTHER'S FASCINATION...

AND IT WORKED... LURING THE SENNA FAMILY IN WITH IT.

THE DERBY GAME WAS THE WARM-UP BEFORE THE SENNAS WOULD HEAD TO CARR AVENUE.

GUY'S CARR AVE FASCINATION WAS RUNNING AT 15 CENTS A PLAY.

WHERE, THE KESSELL BROTHERS HAD BEEN 10 CENTS FOR THE LAST 40 YEARS.

HEY, THERE'S ONLY 48 MACHINES HERE...

THERE WERE 52 AT THE DAVENPORT FASCINATION...

AS RANDY'S RECOGNIZING THE OWNER'S COMPETITIVENESS..

GUY WAS IMPRESSED, AND SAW IN THE SENNA FAMILY AS BEING GOOD FUTURE CUSTOMERS...

EACH FASCINATION MACHINE'S UNIQUE SET OF DIFFERENCES, WOULD ALSO, STAND OUT –

EVEN IF THEY SUPPORTED THE COMPETITION.

RANDY RECOGNIZED GUY'S MACHINES AS BEING FROM THE FORMER DAVENPORT SEASIDE HEIGHTS LOCATION.

FASCINATION, FOR THE YOUNG RANDY – WAS BECOMING A WAY OF LIFE.

IT HAD CLOSED THE TWO SUMMERS BEFORE AND WHILE RANDY FAVORED LUCKY'S, HE ONLY PLAYED THERE ONCE.

..WELL, I'M SURE GLAD MY KENTUCKY DERBY BROUGHT YOU FOLKS HERE..

GO AFTER THE EASY LINES IF YOU HAVE TO!.. GET THE WIN IF YOU CAN'T GET THE BONUS!..

FORGET THE BONUS AND GET THE WIN!!..

Mr. Fascination

DINNNNNNNG!!
SINCE BEFORE YOU WERE BORN
- ALRIGHT!!
FROM LUCKY'S TO DISNEY'S
OH BOY!.. WITH FOUR PLAYERS WITH JUST SIX LEFT ON THE STOPLIGHT - SO CLOSE!..
OUR WINNER -
WITH A PERFECT GAME.. FIVE LEFT ON THE STOP LIGHT!.. LOOK AT YOU!..
CONGRATULATIONS!..
AWARD THAT YOUNG MAN WITH TEN TICKETS!..
ALLL-RIGHT!.. HERE WE GO!..
WITH THREE BALLS NOW,.. COVER YOUR ENTIRE BOARD BEFORE ANYONE ELSE AND GET TWENTY TICKETS PER WIN!..
SPEEDY BINGO!.. COVER-ALL!.. ..READY? HERE - WE - GO!..
Mr. Fascino

DINNNNNNG!!
SINCE BEFORE YOU WERE BORN
THE BEY
AS RANDY RETURNED TO LUCKY'S IN SEASIDE...
GEE, THEY'RE LEAVING ME ALONE TODAY. I'D BETTER KEEP AT IT...
AFTER ALL THE HARASSMENT... AND AFTER THE TWELVE THOUSAND COUPON PAYOUT –
THE FASCINATION OPERATORS HAD COMPLETELY, ALL OF A SUDDEN, STOPPED.
NO ONE WAS BOTHERING TO STOP HIM FROM WINNING OR TELL HIM HE HAD BEEN AT A TABLE TO LONG –
S'YOUR POP GONNA BE AROUND LATER?..
..FREDDIE WANTS TO SPEAK WITH HIM.
LUCKY'S Fascination
LIGHT FIVE
..IT WAS A LIBERATION.
BUT IT WAS ONLY THE CALM BEFORE THE STORM –
THUNDER BEGAN IN THE DISTANCE... AS AN OPERATOR POPPED RANDY A QUESTION –
NOT SAYING HOW LATE, RANDY AND HIS FATHER WOULD END UP WAITING... AND WAITING...
THEN, FREDDIE FINALLY SHOWED UP, AFTER 1 AM...
STAFF ONLY
SO, RANDY..
I HEARD YOU WERE DISCOURTEOUS TO ONE OF MY GIRLS?..

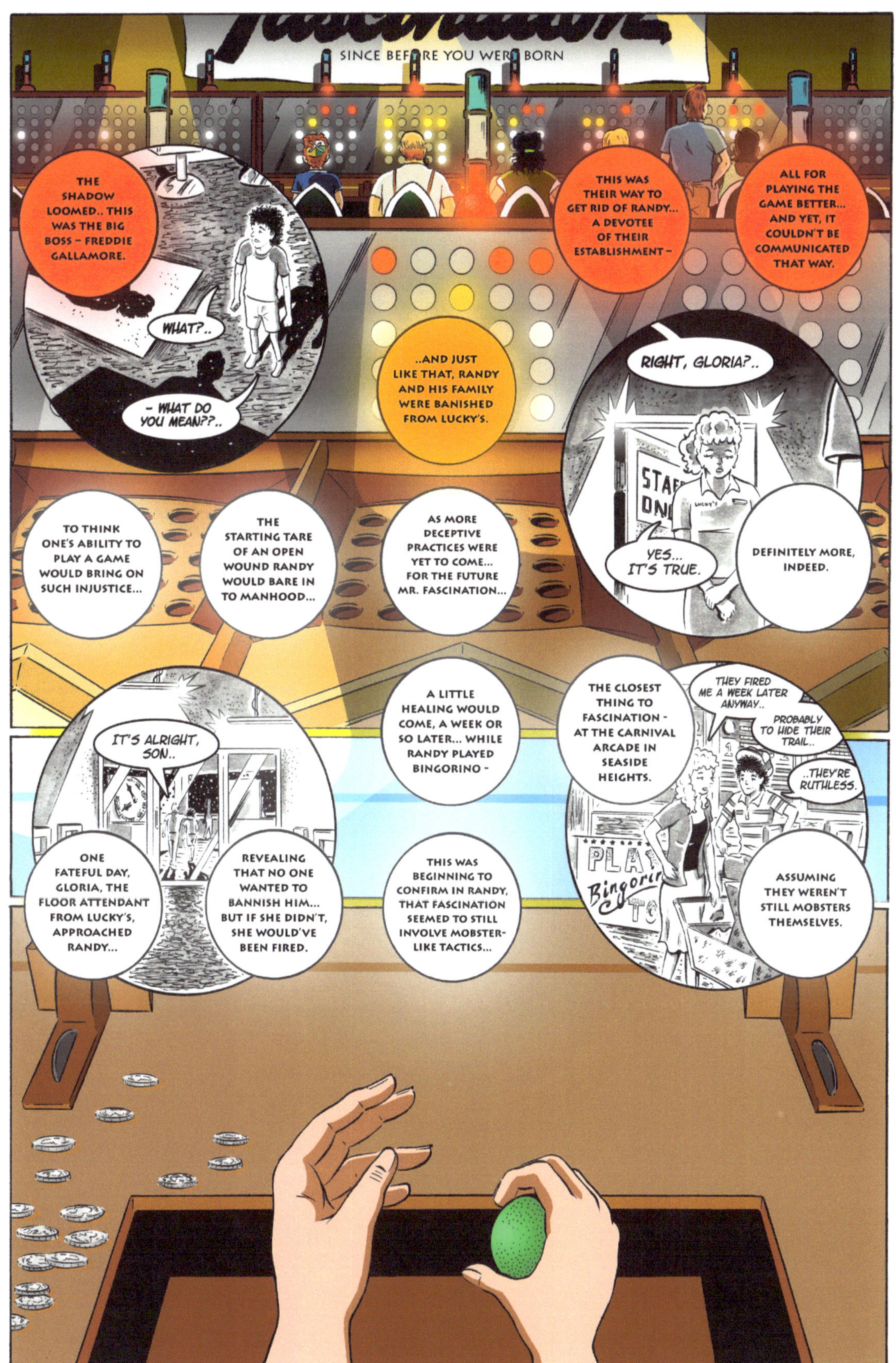
SINCE BEFORE YOU WERE BORN
THE SHADOW LOOMED.. THIS WAS THE BIG BOSS – FREDDIE GALLAMORE.
WHAT?..
– WHAT DO YOU MEAN??..
THIS WAS THEIR WAY TO GET RID OF RANDY... A DEVOTEE OF THEIR ESTABLISHMENT –
ALL FOR PLAYING THE GAME BETTER... AND YET, IT COULDN'T BE COMMUNICATED THAT WAY.
..AND JUST LIKE THAT, RANDY AND HIS FAMILY WERE BANISHED FROM LUCKY'S.
RIGHT, GLORIA?..
YES... IT'S TRUE.
DEFINITELY MORE, INDEED.
TO THINK ONE'S ABILITY TO PLAY A GAME WOULD BRING ON SUCH INJUSTICE...
THE STARTING TARE OF AN OPEN WOUND RANDY WOULD BARE IN TO MANHOOD...
AS MORE DECEPTIVE PRACTICES WERE YET TO COME... FOR THE FUTURE MR. FASCINATION...
IT'S ALRIGHT, SON..
A LITTLE HEALING WOULD COME, A WEEK OR SO LATER... WHILE RANDY PLAYED BINGORINO –
THE CLOSEST THING TO FASCINATION – AT THE CARNIVAL ARCADE IN SEASIDE HEIGHTS.
THEY FIRED ME A WEEK LATER ANYWAY..
PROBABLY TO HIDE THEIR TRAIL..
..THEY'RE RUTHLESS.
ONE FATEFUL DAY, GLORIA, THE FLOOR ATTENDANT FROM LUCKY'S, APPROACHED RANDY...
REVEALING THAT NO ONE WANTED TO BANNISH HIM... BUT IF SHE DIDN'T, SHE WOULD'VE BEEN FIRED.
THIS WAS BEGINNING TO CONFIRM IN RANDY, THAT FASCINATION SEEMED TO STILL INVOLVE MOBSTER-LIKE TACTICS...
ASSUMING THEY WEREN'T STILL MOBSTERS THEMSELVES.

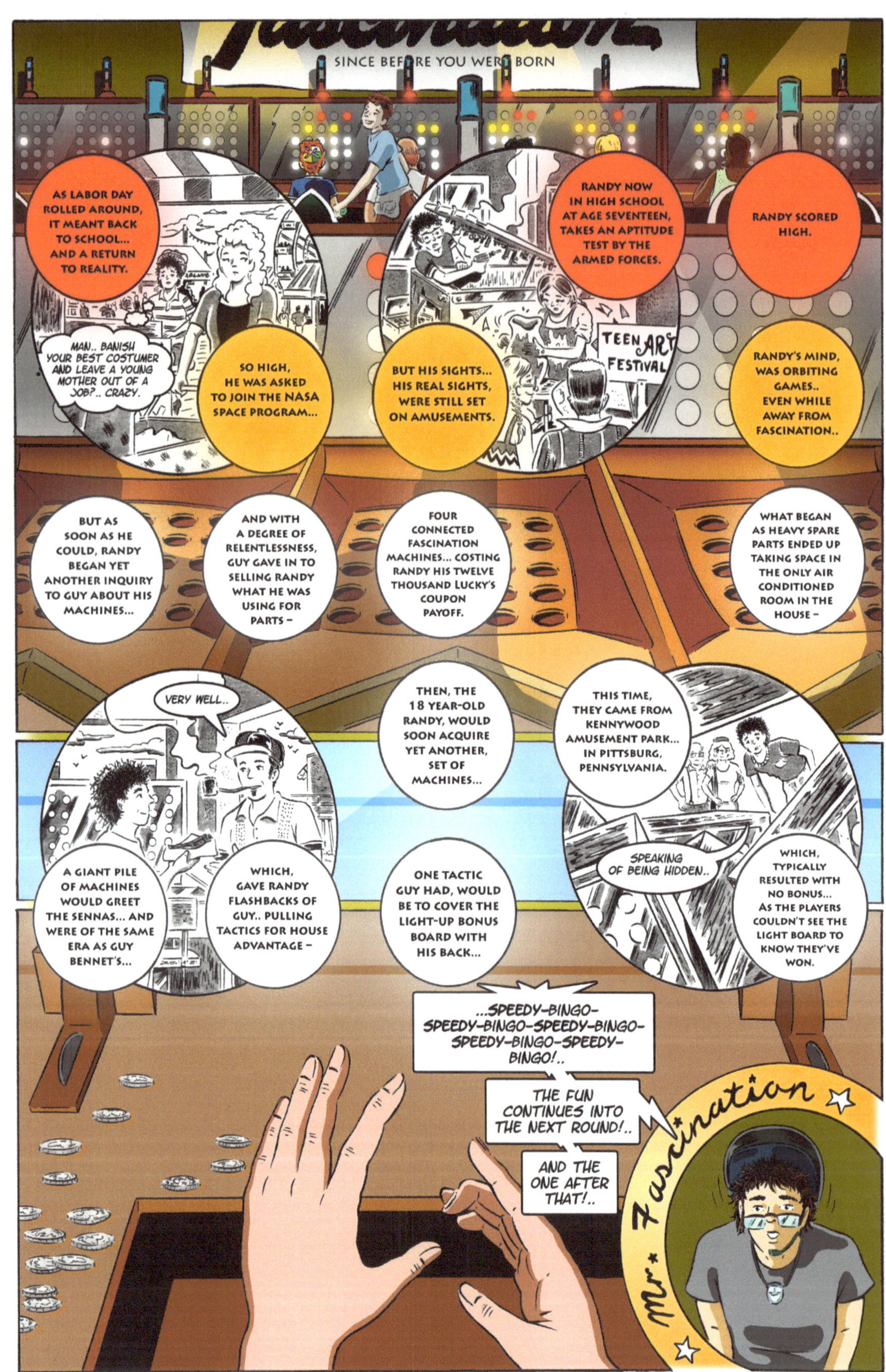
SINCE BEFORE YOU WERE BORN

AS LABOR DAY ROLLED AROUND, IT MEANT BACK TO SCHOOL... AND A RETURN TO REALITY.

MAN.. BANISH YOUR BEST COSTUMER AND LEAVE A YOUNG MOTHER OUT OF A JOB?.. CRAZY.

SO HIGH, HE WAS ASKED TO JOIN THE NASA SPACE PROGRAM...

RANDY NOW IN HIGH SCHOOL AT AGE SEVENTEEN, TAKES AN APTITUDE TEST BY THE ARMED FORCES.

RANDY SCORED HIGH.

BUT HIS SIGHTS... HIS REAL SIGHTS, WERE STILL SET ON AMUSEMENTS.

TEEN ART FESTIVAL

RANDY'S MIND, WAS ORBITING GAMES.. EVEN WHILE AWAY FROM FASCINATION..

BUT AS SOON AS HE COULD, RANDY BEGAN YET ANOTHER INQUIRY TO GUY ABOUT HIS MACHINES...

AND WITH A DEGREE OF RELENTLESSNESS, GUY GAVE IN TO SELLING RANDY WHAT HE WAS USING FOR PARTS –

FOUR CONNECTED FASCINATION MACHINES... COSTING RANDY HIS TWELVE THOUSAND LUCKY'S COUPON PAYOFF.

WHAT BEGAN AS HEAVY SPARE PARTS ENDED UP TAKING SPACE IN THE ONLY AIR CONDITIONED ROOM IN THE HOUSE –

VERY WELL..

THEN, THE 18 YEAR-OLD RANDY, WOULD SOON ACQUIRE YET ANOTHER, SET OF MACHINES...

THIS TIME, THEY CAME FROM KENNYWOOD AMUSEMENT PARK... IN PITTSBURG, PENNSYLVANIA.

A GIANT PILE OF MACHINES WOULD GREET THE SENNAS... AND WERE OF THE SAME ERA AS GUY BENNET'S...

WHICH, GAVE RANDY FLASHBACKS OF GUY.. PULLING TACTICS FOR HOUSE ADVANTAGE –

ONE TACTIC GUY HAD, WOULD BE TO COVER THE LIGHT-UP BONUS BOARD WITH HIS BACK...

SPEAKING OF BEING HIDDEN..

WHICH, TYPICALLY RESULTED WITH NO BONUS... AS THE PLAYERS COULDN'T SEE THE LIGHT BOARD TO KNOW THEY'VE WON.

...SPEEDY-BINGO-SPEEDY-BINGO-SPEEDY-BINGO-SPEEDY-BINGO-SPEEDY-BINGO!..

THE FUN CONTINUES INTO THE NEXT ROUND!..

AND THE ONE AFTER THAT!..

Mr. Fascination

THE BELL
DINNNNNNG!!
SINCE BEFORE YOU WERE BORN
- YES!..
MORE ACQUISTIONS
- AND WE HAVE OUR WINNER OF OUR FIRST SPEEDY BINGO ROUND!.. CONGRATULATIONS!..
WITH THE ADDITION OF YET ANOTHER EXTRA BALL, LET'S ROLLLLL-EM' AGAIN!..
READY??..
Mr. Fascination

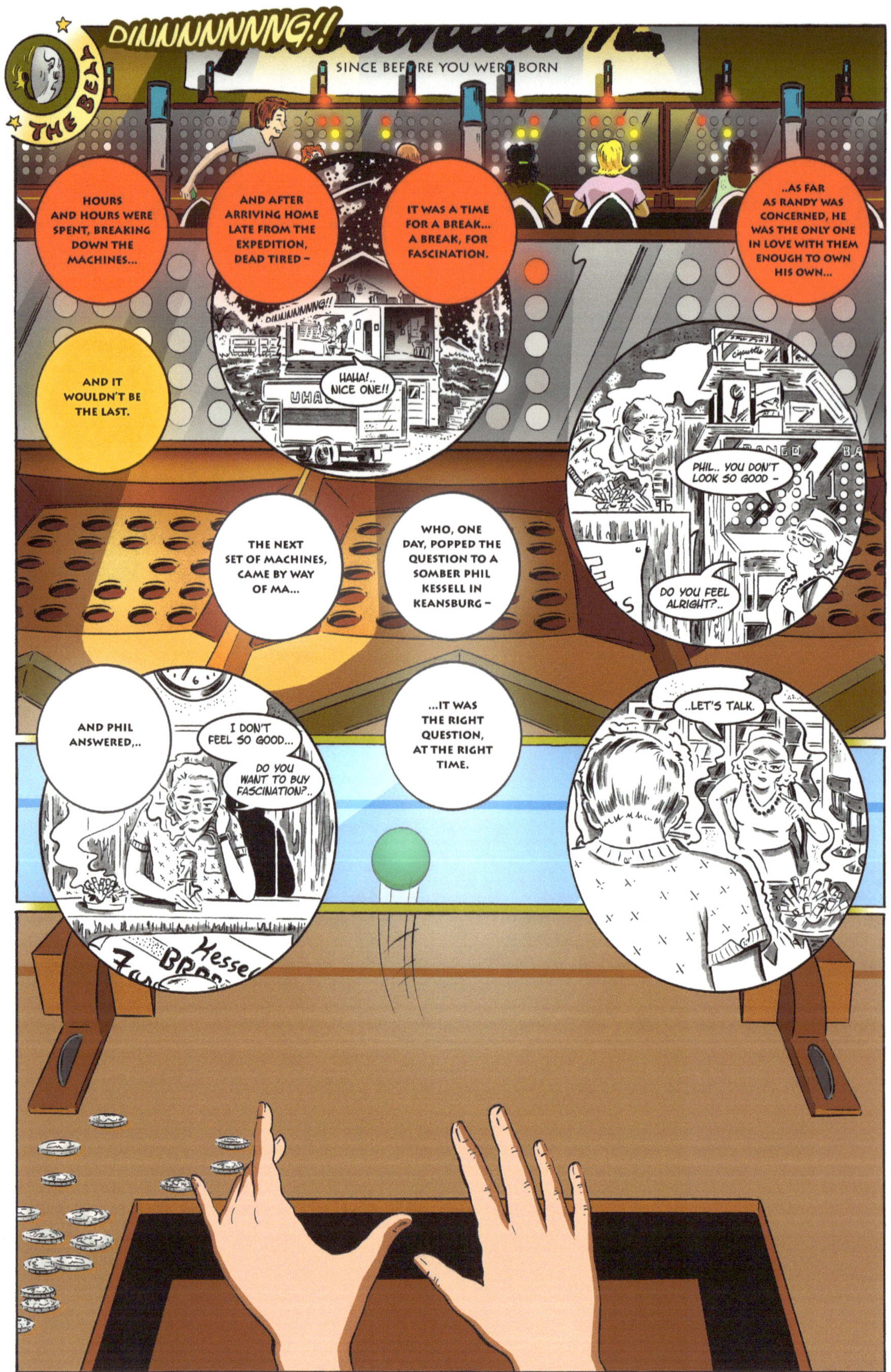

DINNNNNNNG!!
THE BEAT
SINCE BEFORE YOU WERE BORN
HOURS AND HOURS WERE SPENT, BREAKING DOWN THE MACHINES...
AND AFTER ARRIVING HOME LATE FROM THE EXPEDITION, DEAD TIRED –
IT WAS A TIME FOR A BREAK... A BREAK, FOR FASCINATION.
..AS FAR AS RANDY WAS CONCERNED, HE WAS THE ONLY ONE IN LOVE WITH THEM ENOUGH TO OWN HIS OWN...
AND IT WOULDN'T BE THE LAST.
DINNNNNNNG!!
HAHA!.. NICE ONE!!
UHA
THE NEXT SET OF MACHINES, CAME BY WAY OF MA...
WHO, ONE DAY, POPPED THE QUESTION TO A SOMBER PHIL KESSELL IN KEANSBURG –
PHIL.. YOU DON'T LOOK SO GOOD –
DO YOU FEEL ALRIGHT?..
AND PHIL ANSWERED,...
I DON'T FEEL SO GOOD...
DO YOU WANT TO BUY FASCINATION?..
...IT WAS THE RIGHT QUESTION, AT THE RIGHT TIME.
..LET'S TALK.
Kessel
BRRR
30

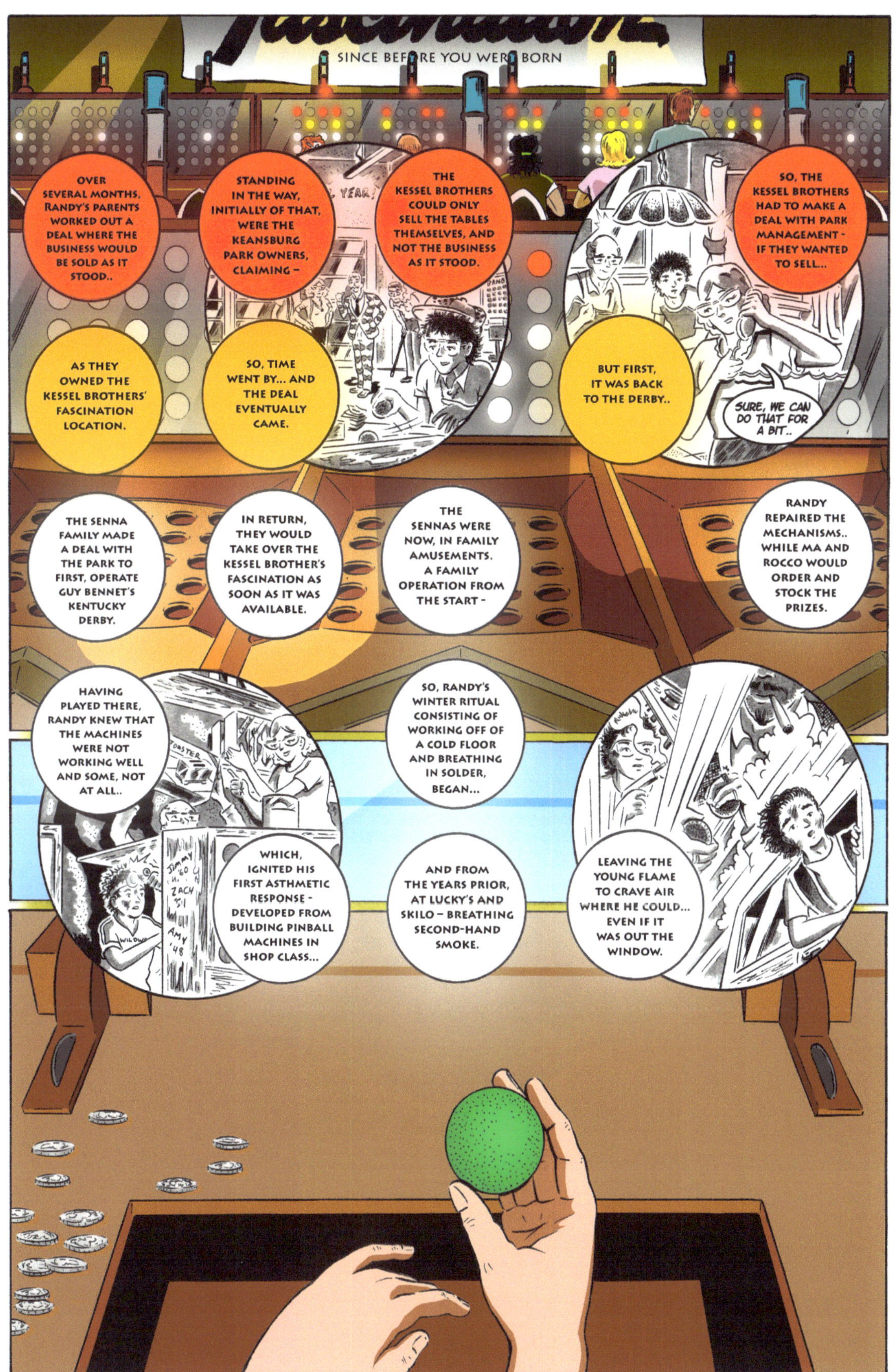
FASCINATION
SINCE BEFORE YOU WERE BORN

OVER SEVERAL MONTHS, RANDY'S PARENTS WORKED OUT A DEAL WHERE THE BUSINESS WOULD BE SOLD AS IT STOOD..

STANDING IN THE WAY, INITIALLY OF THAT, WERE THE KEANSBURG PARK OWNERS, CLAIMING -

THE KESSEL BROTHERS COULD ONLY SELL THE TABLES THEMSELVES, AND NOT THE BUSINESS AS IT STOOD.

SO, THE KESSEL BROTHERS HAD TO MAKE A DEAL WITH PARK MANAGEMENT - IF THEY WANTED TO SELL...

AS THEY OWNED THE KESSEL BROTHERS' FASCINATION LOCATION.

SO, TIME WENT BY... AND THE DEAL EVENTUALLY CAME.

BUT FIRST, IT WAS BACK TO THE DERBY..

SURE, WE CAN DO THAT FOR A BIT..

THE SENNA FAMILY MADE A DEAL WITH THE PARK TO FIRST, OPERATE GUY BENNET'S KENTUCKY DERBY.

IN RETURN, THEY WOULD TAKE OVER THE KESSEL BROTHER'S FASCINATION AS SOON AS IT WAS AVAILABLE.

THE SENNAS WERE NOW, IN FAMILY AMUSEMENTS. A FAMILY OPERATION FROM THE START -

RANDY REPAIRED THE MECHANISMS.. WHILE MA AND ROCCO WOULD ORDER AND STOCK THE PRIZES.

HAVING PLAYED THERE, RANDY KNEW THAT THE MACHINES WERE NOT WORKING WELL AND SOME, NOT AT ALL..

SO, RANDY'S WINTER RITUAL CONSISTING OF WORKING OFF OF A COLD FLOOR AND BREATHING IN SOLDER, BEGAN...

WHICH, IGNITED HIS FIRST ASTHMETIC RESPONSE - DEVELOPED FROM BUILDING PINBALL MACHINES IN SHOP CLASS...

AND FROM THE YEARS PRIOR, AT LUCKY'S AND SKILO - BREATHING SECOND-HAND SMOKE.

LEAVING THE YOUNG FLAME TO CRAVE AIR WHERE HE COULD... EVEN IF IT WAS OUT THE WINDOW.

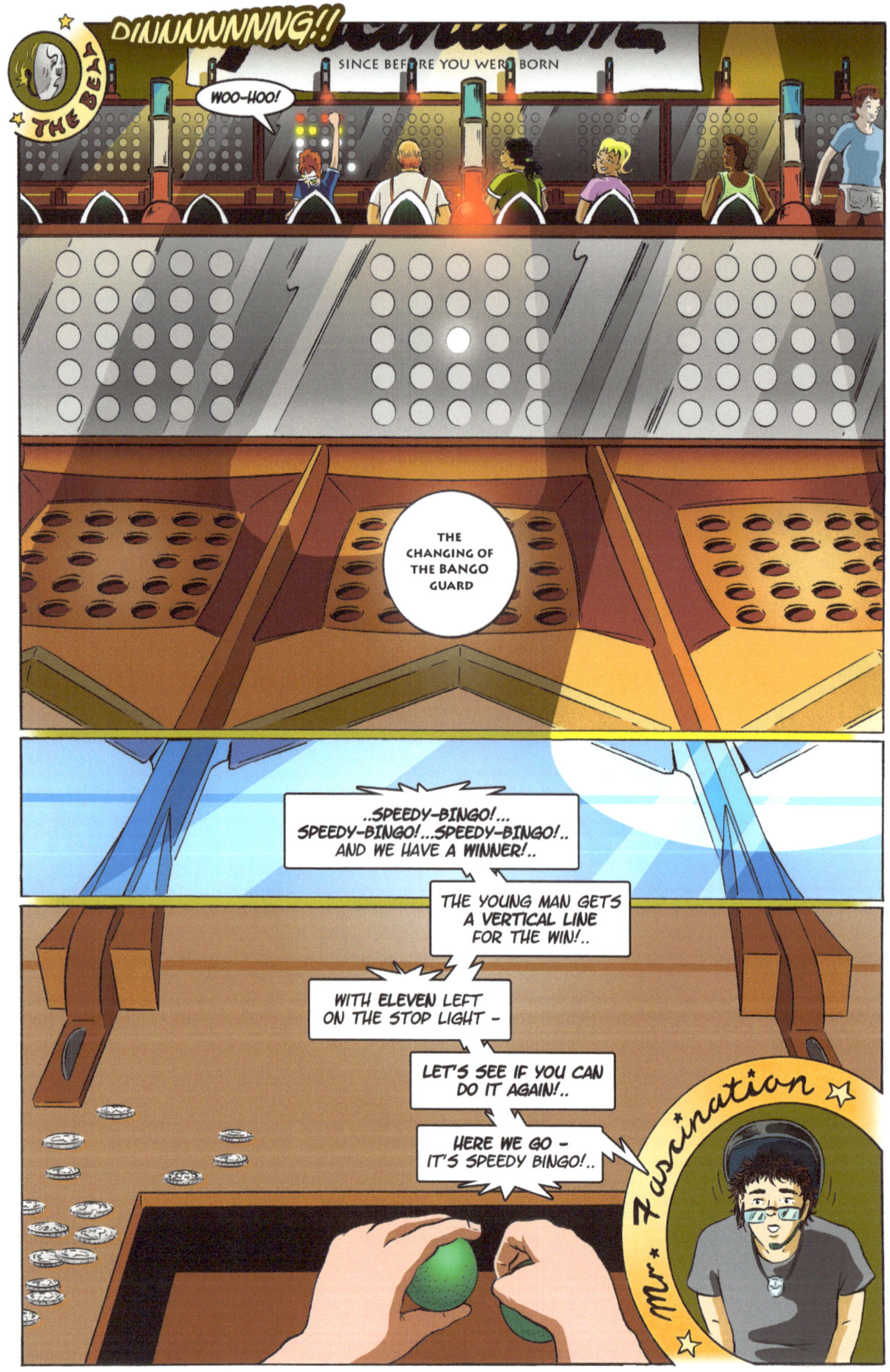
THE BEST
DINNNNNNNG!!
SINCE BEFORE YOU WERE BORN
WOO-HOO!
THE CHANGING OF THE BANGO GUARD
..SPEEDY-BINGO!...
SPEEDY-BINGO!...SPEEDY-BINGO!..
AND WE HAVE A WINNER!..
THE YOUNG MAN GETS A VERTICAL LINE FOR THE WIN!..
WITH ELEVEN LEFT ON THE STOP LIGHT -
LET'S SEE IF YOU CAN DO IT AGAIN!..
HERE WE GO - IT'S SPEEDY BINGO!..
Mr. Fascination

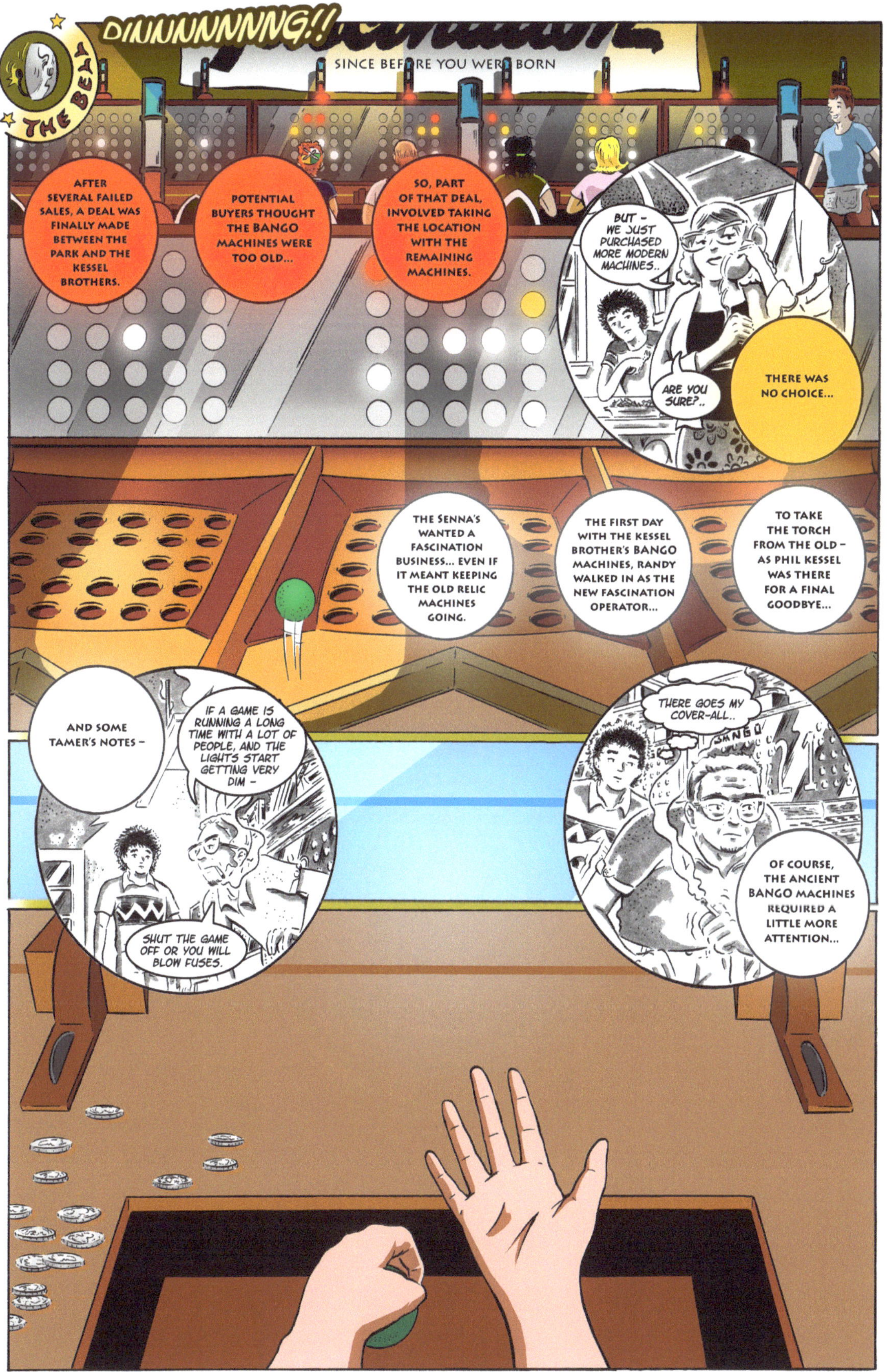

DINNNNNNG!!
SINCE BEFORE YOU WERE BORN
THE DEAL
AFTER SEVERAL FAILED SALES, A DEAL WAS FINALLY MADE BETWEEN THE PARK AND THE KESSEL BROTHERS.
POTENTIAL BUYERS THOUGHT THE BANGO MACHINES WERE TOO OLD...
SO, PART OF THAT DEAL, INVOLVED TAKING THE LOCATION WITH THE REMAINING MACHINES.
BUT — WE JUST PURCHASED MORE MODERN MACHINES..
ARE YOU SURE?..
THERE WAS NO CHOICE...
THE SENNA'S WANTED A FASCINATION BUSINESS... EVEN IF IT MEANT KEEPING THE OLD RELIC MACHINES GOING.
THE FIRST DAY WITH THE KESSEL BROTHER'S BANGO MACHINES, RANDY WALKED IN AS THE NEW FASCINATION OPERATOR...
TO TAKE THE TORCH FROM THE OLD — AS PHIL KESSEL WAS THERE FOR A FINAL GOODBYE...
AND SOME TAMER'S NOTES —
IF A GAME IS RUNNING A LONG TIME WITH A LOT OF PEOPLE, AND THE LIGHTS START GETTING VERY DIM —
SHUT THE GAME OFF OR YOU WILL BLOW FUSES.
THERE GOES MY COVER-ALL..
BANGO
OF COURSE, THE ANCIENT BANGO MACHINES REQUIRED A LITTLE MORE ATTENTION...

33

SINCE BEFORE YOU WERE BORN
AS PHIL LEAD RANDY TOWARD THE GIANT GARAGE DOOR'S ACCESS EXIT...
HE STOPPED FOR A MOMENT, AND TURNED BACK TO LOOK AT RANDY FOR THE FINAL TIME.
WITH A LOOK OF SADNESS OVER HIM, HE SAID,...
LET'S NOT LET IT END LIKE THIS...
AND JUST LIKE THAT - PHIL KESSEL VANISHED.
BEST OF LUCK WITH IT.
IT WAS AN EERIE FEELING FOR RANDY... LOCKING THE DOORS BEHIND THE CARETAKER FOR THE LAST 40 YEARS...
A MOMENT THAT HAD TO EVENTUALLY COME.. A CHANGING OF THE GUARD.
RANDY FIRST TOOK TO EXPLORING THE BACK ROOMS... WHICH, BROUGHT DISCOVERIES —
AND EVEN, CONFIRMED SOME TRUTHS... AS THE KESSEL BROTHERS TOO, HAD A MAFIA-TYPE LAYOUT GOING...
RANDY ENDED UP FINDING A HIDDEN BATHROOM, OFFICE AND A THIN HIDE-A-WAY, BEHIND A FALSE WALL...
HELLO?.. ANYONE BACK HERE?..
AND BECAUSE THE KESSEL BROTHERS DIDN'T OFFER MERCHANDISE PRIZES, WHAT REMAINED WERE REMNANTS —
DISPLAYS OF EMPTY BOXES OF CIGARETTE CARTONS, BAKING DISHES, AND PIGGY BANKS...
ALL KEPT TO BUILD A FASSAD... BUT RANDY, WAS FAR FROM FAKE.
GRAB A SEAT, GRAB A BALL, TIME TO PLAY, IT'S TIME TO WIN!!..

34

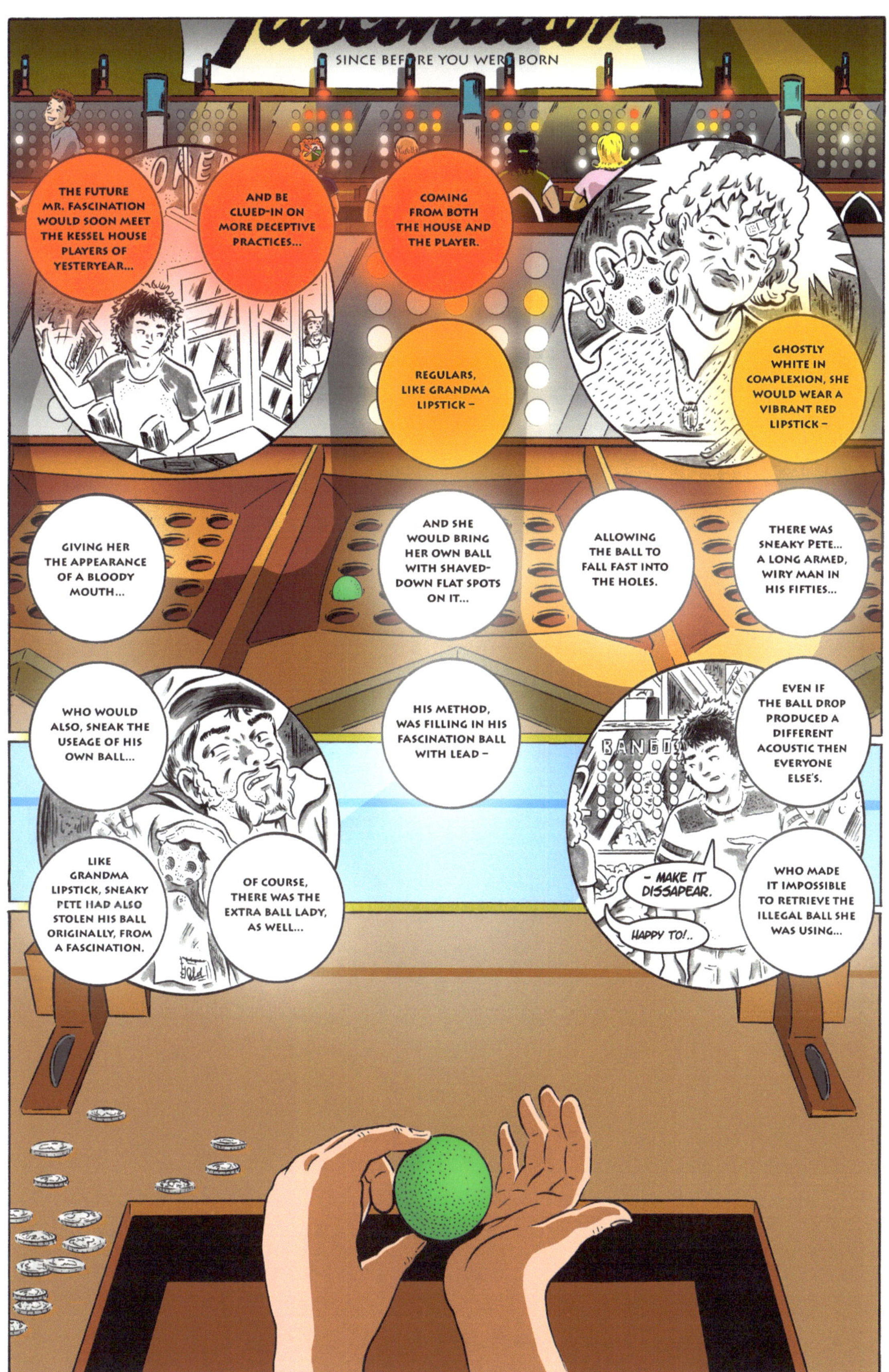

FASCINATION
SINCE BEFORE YOU WERE BORN

THE FUTURE MR. FASCINATION WOULD SOON MEET THE KESSEL HOUSE PLAYERS OF YESTERYEAR...

AND BE CLUED-IN ON MORE DECEPTIVE PRACTICES...

COMING FROM BOTH THE HOUSE AND THE PLAYER.

REGULARS, LIKE GRANDMA LIPSTICK –

GHOSTLY WHITE IN COMPLEXION, SHE WOULD WEAR A VIBRANT RED LIPSTICK –

GIVING HER THE APPEARANCE OF A BLOODY MOUTH...

AND SHE WOULD BRING HER OWN BALL WITH SHAVED-DOWN FLAT SPOTS ON IT...

ALLOWING THE BALL TO FALL FAST INTO THE HOLES.

THERE WAS SNEAKY PETE... A LONG ARMED, WIRY MAN IN HIS FIFTIES...

WHO WOULD ALSO, SNEAK THE USEAGE OF HIS OWN BALL...

HIS METHOD, WAS FILLING IN HIS FASCINATION BALL WITH LEAD –

EVEN IF THE BALL DROP PRODUCED A DIFFERENT ACOUSTIC THEN EVERYONE ELSE'S.

BANGO

– MAKE IT DISSAPEAR.

HAPPY TO!..

LIKE GRANDMA LIPSTICK, SNEAKY PETE HAD ALSO STOLEN HIS BALL ORIGINALLY, FROM A FASCINATION.

OF COURSE, THERE WAS THE EXTRA BALL LADY, AS WELL...

WHO MADE IT IMPOSSIBLE TO RETRIEVE THE ILLEGAL BALL SHE WAS USING...

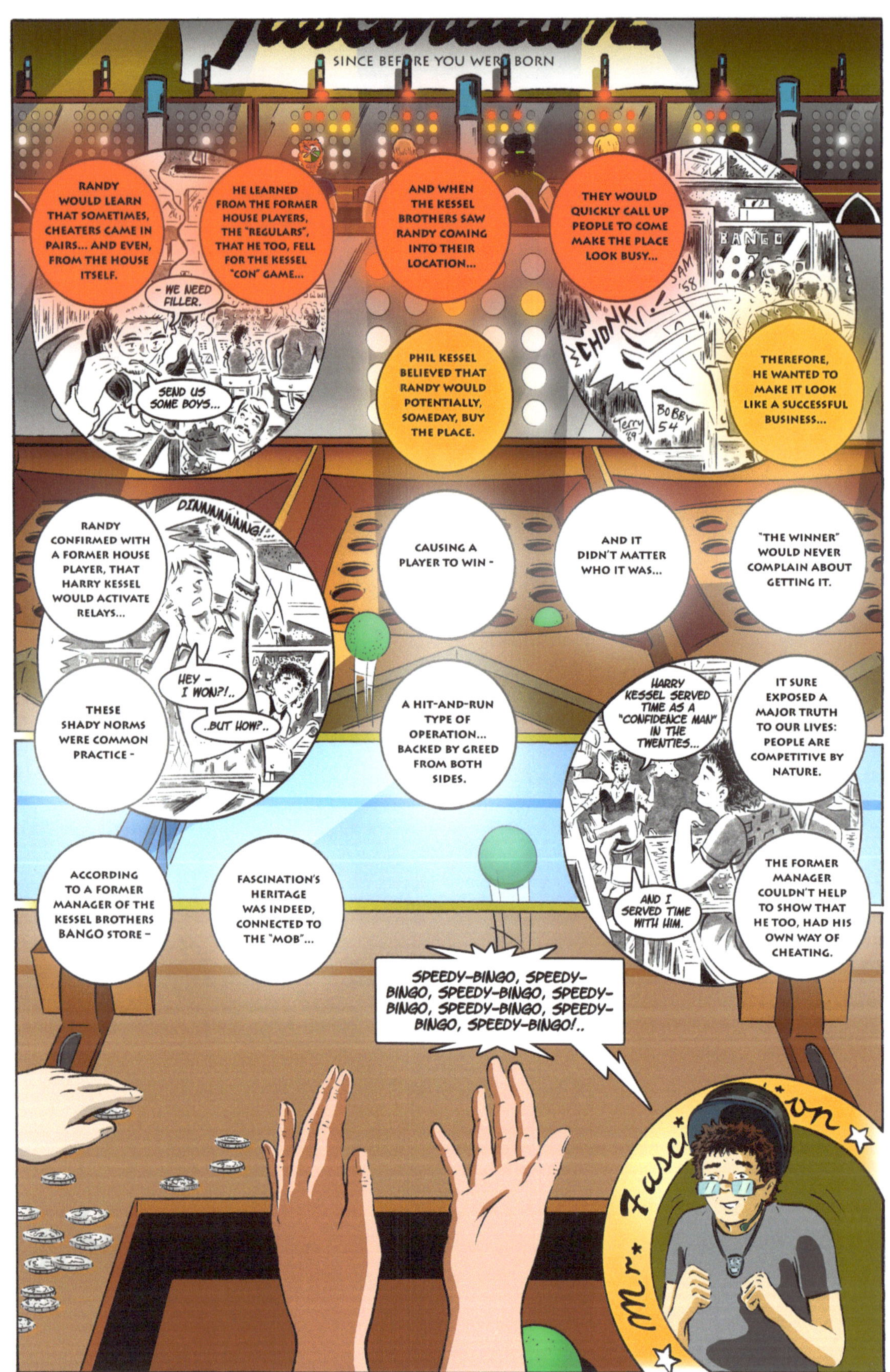

SINCE BEFORE YOU WERE BORN
RANDY WOULD LEARN THAT SOMETIMES, CHEATERS CAME IN PAIRS... AND EVEN, FROM THE HOUSE ITSELF.
HE LEARNED FROM THE FORMER HOUSE PLAYERS, THE "REGULARS", THAT HE TOO, FELL FOR THE KESSEL "CON" GAME...
AND WHEN THE KESSEL BROTHERS SAW RANDY COMING INTO THEIR LOCATION...
THEY WOULD QUICKLY CALL UP PEOPLE TO COME MAKE THE PLACE LOOK BUSY...
- WE NEED FILLER.
SEND US SOME BOYS...
PHIL KESSEL BELIEVED THAT RANDY WOULD POTENTIALLY, SOMEDAY, BUY THE PLACE.
THEREFORE, HE WANTED TO MAKE IT LOOK LIKE A SUCCESSFUL BUSINESS...
RANDY CONFIRMED WITH A FORMER HOUSE PLAYER, THAT HARRY KESSEL WOULD ACTIVATE RELAYS...
DINNNNNNNG!...
HEY - I WON?!..
..BUT HOW?.
CAUSING A PLAYER TO WIN -
AND IT DIDN'T MATTER WHO IT WAS...
"THE WINNER" WOULD NEVER COMPLAIN ABOUT GETTING IT.
THESE SHADY NORMS WERE COMMON PRACTICE -
A HIT-AND-RUN TYPE OF OPERATION... BACKED BY GREED FROM BOTH SIDES.
HARRY KESSEL SERVED TIME AS A "CONFIDENCE MAN" IN THE TWENTIES...
IT SURE EXPOSED A MAJOR TRUTH TO OUR LIVES: PEOPLE ARE COMPETITIVE BY NATURE.
ACCORDING TO A FORMER MANAGER OF THE KESSEL BROTHERS BANGO STORE -
FASCINATION'S HERITAGE WAS INDEED, CONNECTED TO THE "MOB"...
AND I SERVED TIME WITH HIM.
THE FORMER MANAGER COULDN'T HELP TO SHOW THAT HE TOO, HAD HIS OWN WAY OF CHEATING.
SPEEDY-BINGO, SPEEDY-BINGO, SPEEDY-BINGO, SPEEDY-BINGO, SPEEDY-BINGO, SPEEDY-BINGO, SPEEDY-BINGO!..
Mr. Fascination

SINCE BEFORE YOU WERE BORN

HIS FAVORITE TABLE, AS HE SHOWS RANDY, HAD TAKEN THE WEAR AND TEAR WITH "KNEE-LIFTS".

LIFTING THE FASCINATION TABLE BY THE BALLS OF THE FEET, ALLOWED FOR A MORE ACCURATE AIM –

LEVELING-OUT THE FASCINATION PLAYING FIELD... AS THE HOUSE WAS CHEATING TOO.

IT WAS ALL NO MATTER TO RANDY, A DARK PAST OR NOT – HIS DREAM HAD BEEN ACHIEVED.

MISTER, EVEN WITH KNOWING ALL OF THIS, FASCINATION IS MORE THAN A GAME TO ME..

THE THREE-PIECE SUIT TRADITION OF HARRY KESSEL WOULD LIVE ON... THAT IS, UNTIL RANDY RUINED THEM.

..AND RANDY WOULD PROVE IT. FIRST, PAYING TRIBUTE TO THE KESSEL BROTHERS –

NICE SUIT AND 'STASH, RANDY.

THE TAMER OF THE CROWD AND THE TAMER OF THE MACHINE, PROVED TO BE A DIFFICULT JOB SIMULTANEOUSLY –

AS THERE WAS NO WAY TO TEND BOTH THE CONTROL BOOTH AND COLLECT THE COINS...

THE 1938 MACHINES REQUIRED RANDY TO QUICKLY RETURN TO THE BOOTH FOR A RESTART.

AN EXHAUSTING ACT, DONE UNTIL THE 18 YEAR-OLD DECIDED TO MAKE HIS OWN TRANSMITTER.

THE FIRST WIRELESS MICROPHONE FOR AMUSEMENT GAMES WAS DEVELOPED...

DIII–IIIIIINNNG!!...

AND IT CAME, ONCE AGAIN, OUT OF RANDY'S ELECTRO-MECHANICAL ENGENUITY.

ONE COULD NOW, TRANSMIT HIS OR HER VOICE FROM A WALKIE TALKIE TO A CB RADIO, THEN TO A PA SYSTEM..

RANDY WOULD ALSO DEVELOP A REMOTE START CONTROLLER, USING A GARAGE DOOR RADIO FREQUENCY DEVICE.

DURING THIS TIME, EVEN WITH HIS LEVEL OF MECHANICAL ELECTRONICS MASTERY...

IF THERE WAS ONE THING RANDY WANTED FROM THE BANGO MACHINES...

ALRIGHT,... LET'S PLAY IT AGAIN!.. HERE WE GO!..

IT WAS THE ADDITION OF THE GAME CALLED "COVER-ALL"... A.K.A. "SPEEDY BINGO."

SPEEDY-BINGO, SPEEDY-BINGO, SPEEDY-BINGO, SPEEDY-BINGO, SPEEDY-BINGO, SPEEDY-BINGO, SPEEDY-BINGO!..

Mr. Fascina

THE BEAT
DINNNNNNNG!!
SINCE BEFORE YOU WERE BORN
YESSS!..
THE FIRES
- AND HE'S HEATING UP!!..
DON'T PASS IT BY... GIVE IT A TRY!..
IT'S EASY, IT'S FUN, IT'S FASCINATION!..
LET'S PLAY SOME MORE SPEEDY BINGO!.. HERE WE GO!!..
Mr. Fascination

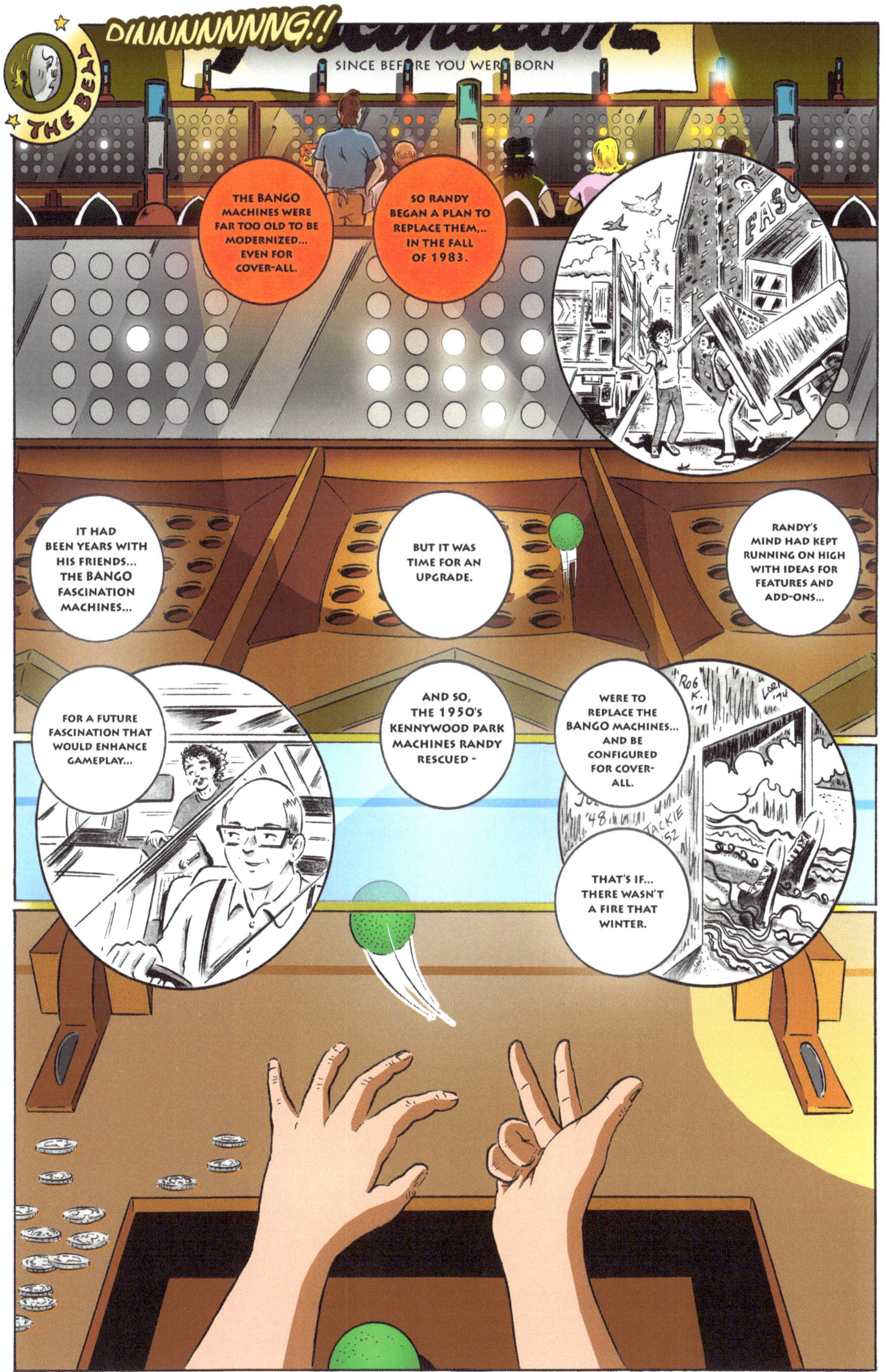

DINNNNNNG!!
THE BEAT
SINCE BEFORE YOU WERE BORN
THE BANGO MACHINES WERE FAR TOO OLD TO BE MODERNIZED... EVEN FOR COVER-ALL.
SO RANDY BEGAN A PLAN TO REPLACE THEM,... IN THE FALL OF 1983.
IT HAD BEEN YEARS WITH HIS FRIENDS... THE BANGO FASCINATION MACHINES...
BUT IT WAS TIME FOR AN UPGRADE.
RANDY'S MIND HAD KEPT RUNNING ON HIGH WITH IDEAS FOR FEATURES AND ADD-ONS...
FOR A FUTURE FASCINATION THAT WOULD ENHANCE GAMEPLAY...
AND SO, THE 1950's KENNYWOOD PARK MACHINES RANDY RESCUED -
WERE TO REPLACE THE BANGO MACHINES... AND BE CONFIGURED FOR COVER-ALL.
THAT'S IF... THERE WASN'T A FIRE THAT WINTER.

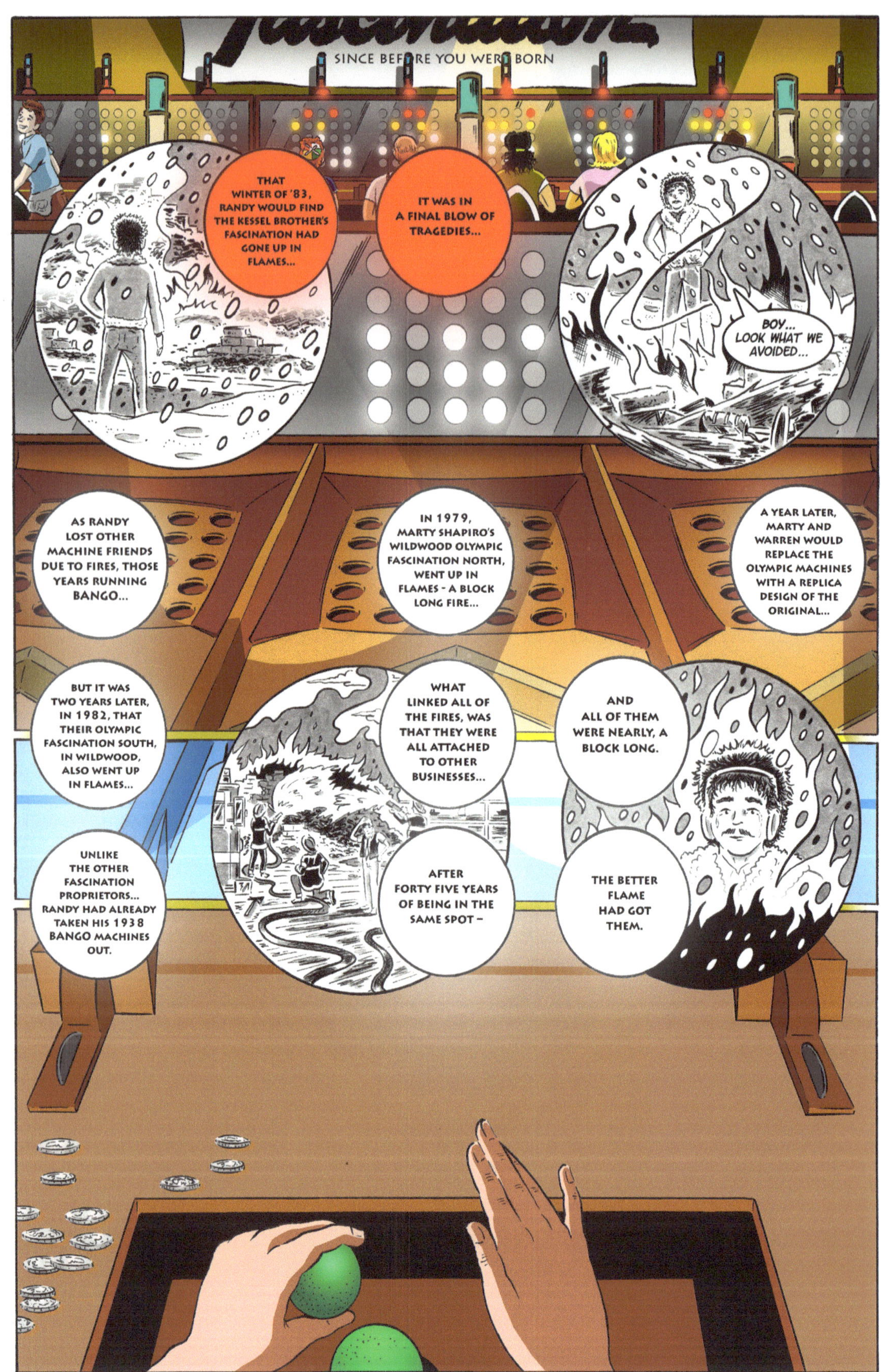
SINCE BEFORE YOU WERE BORN
THAT WINTER OF '83, RANDY WOULD FIND THE KESSEL BROTHER'S FASCINATION HAD GONE UP IN FLAMES...
IT WAS IN A FINAL BLOW OF TRAGEDIES...
BOY... LOOK WHAT WE AVOIDED...
AS RANDY LOST OTHER MACHINE FRIENDS DUE TO FIRES, THOSE YEARS RUNNING BANGO...
IN 1979, MARTY SHAPIRO'S WILDWOOD OLYMPIC FASCINATION NORTH, WENT UP IN FLAMES - A BLOCK LONG FIRE...
A YEAR LATER, MARTY AND WARREN WOULD REPLACE THE OLYMPIC MACHINES WITH A REPLICA DESIGN OF THE ORIGINAL...
BUT IT WAS TWO YEARS LATER, IN 1982, THAT THEIR OLYMPIC FASCINATION SOUTH, IN WILDWOOD, ALSO WENT UP IN FLAMES...
WHAT LINKED ALL OF THE FIRES, WAS THAT THEY WERE ALL ATTACHED TO OTHER BUSINESSES...
AND ALL OF THEM WERE NEARLY, A BLOCK LONG.
UNLIKE THE OTHER FASCINATION PROPRIETORS... RANDY HAD ALREADY TAKEN HIS 1938 BANGO MACHINES OUT.
AFTER FORTY FIVE YEARS OF BEING IN THE SAME SPOT –
THE BETTER FLAME HAD GOT THEM.

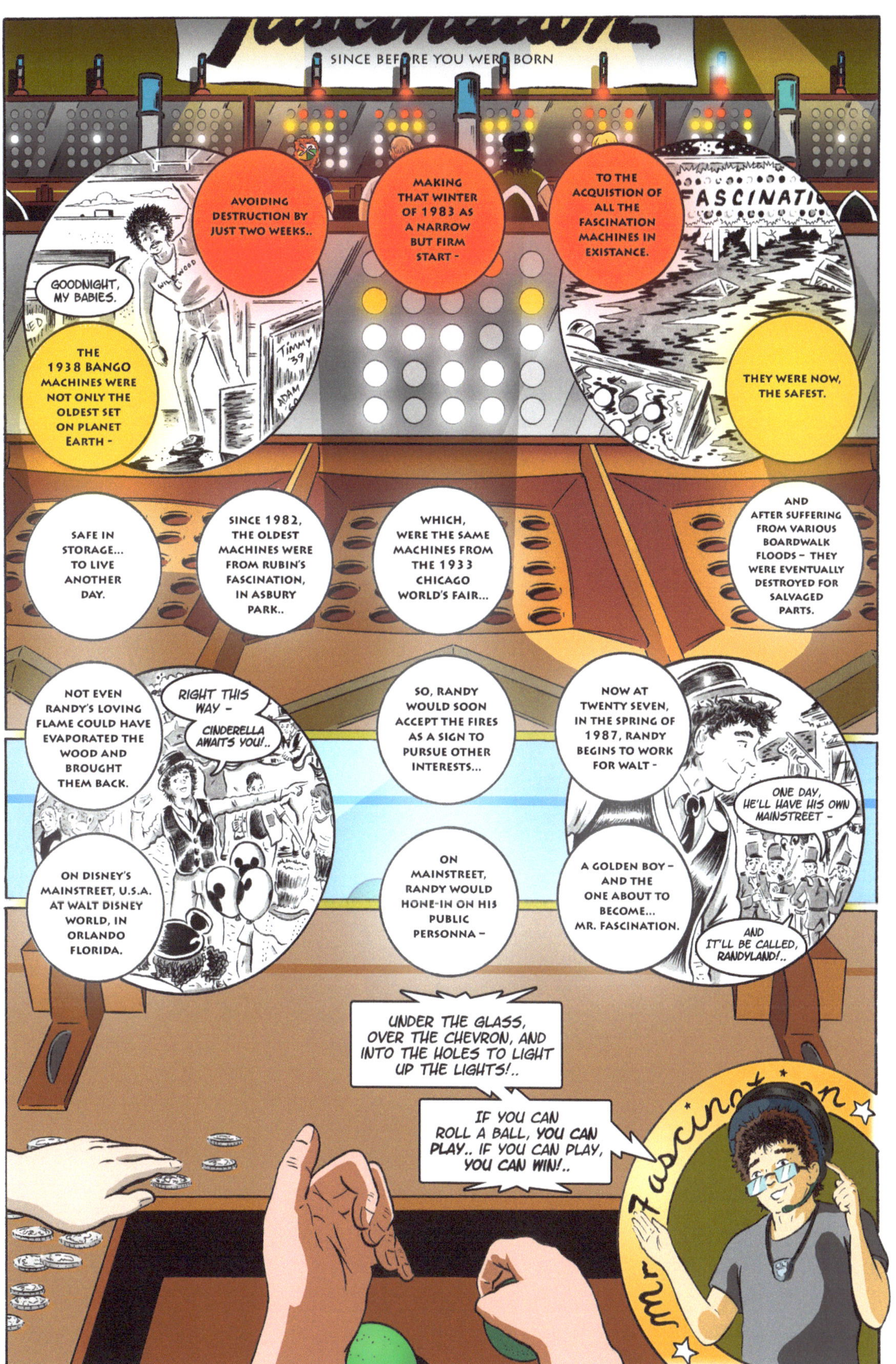
FASCINATION
SINCE BEFORE YOU WERE BORN
GOODNIGHT, MY BABIES.
AVOIDING DESTRUCTION BY JUST TWO WEEKS..
MAKING THAT WINTER OF 1983 AS A NARROW BUT FIRM START -
TO THE ACQUISTION OF ALL THE FASCINATION MACHINES IN EXISTANCE.
THE 1938 BANGO MACHINES WERE NOT ONLY THE OLDEST SET ON PLANET EARTH -
THEY WERE NOW, THE SAFEST.
SAFE IN STORAGE... TO LIVE ANOTHER DAY.
SINCE 1982, THE OLDEST MACHINES WERE FROM RUBIN'S FASCINATION, IN ASBURY PARK..
WHICH, WERE THE SAME MACHINES FROM THE 1933 CHICAGO WORLD'S FAIR...
AND AFTER SUFFERING FROM VARIOUS BOARDWALK FLOODS - THEY WERE EVENTUALLY DESTROYED FOR SALVAGED PARTS.
NOT EVEN RANDY'S LOVING FLAME COULD HAVE EVAPORATED THE WOOD AND BROUGHT THEM BACK.
RIGHT THIS WAY -
- CINDERELLA AWAITS YOU!..
SO, RANDY WOULD SOON ACCEPT THE FIRES AS A SIGN TO PURSUE OTHER INTERESTS...
NOW AT TWENTY SEVEN, IN THE SPRING OF 1987, RANDY BEGINS TO WORK FOR WALT -
ONE DAY, HE'LL HAVE HIS OWN MAINSTREET -
ON DISNEY'S MAINSTREET, U.S.A. AT WALT DISNEY WORLD, IN ORLANDO FLORIDA.
ON MAINSTREET, RANDY WOULD HONE-IN ON HIS PUBLIC PERSONNA -
A GOLDEN BOY - AND THE ONE ABOUT TO BECOME... MR. FASCINATION.
AND IT'LL BE CALLED, RANDYLAND!..
UNDER THE GLASS, OVER THE CHEVRON, AND INTO THE HOLES TO LIGHT UP THE LIGHTS!..
IF YOU CAN ROLL A BALL, YOU CAN PLAY.. IF YOU CAN PLAY, YOU CAN WIN!..
Mr. Fascination

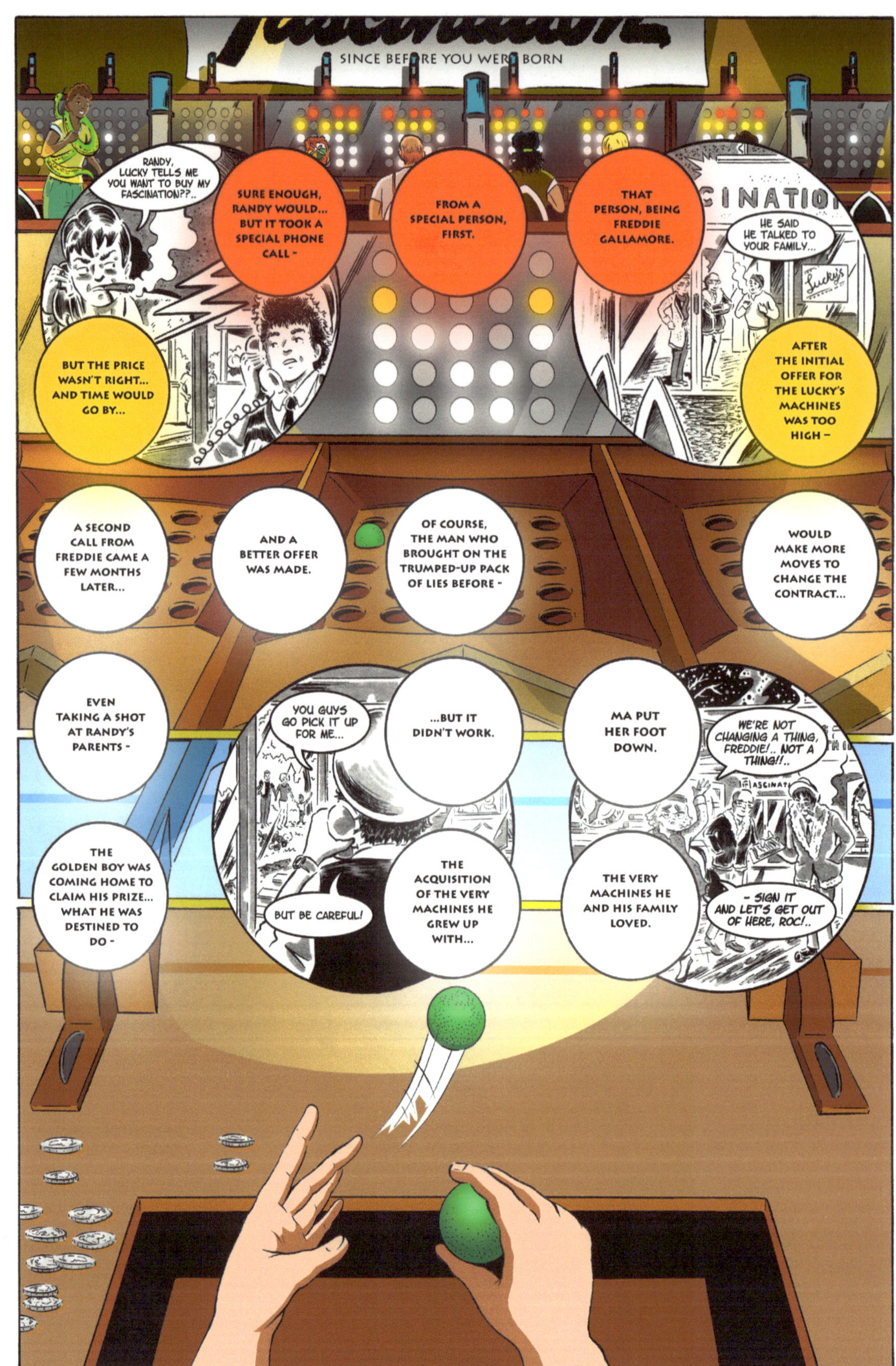
FASCINATION
SINCE BEFORE YOU WERE BORN
RANDY, LUCKY TELLS ME YOU WANT TO BUY MY FASCINATION??..
SURE ENOUGH, RANDY WOULD... BUT IT TOOK A SPECIAL PHONE CALL –
FROM A SPECIAL PERSON, FIRST.
THAT PERSON, BEING FREDDIE GALLAMORE.
HE SAID HE TALKED TO YOUR FAMILY...
LUCKY'S
BUT THE PRICE WASN'T RIGHT... AND TIME WOULD GO BY...
CINATION
AFTER THE INITIAL OFFER FOR THE LUCKY'S MACHINES WAS TOO HIGH –
A SECOND CALL FROM FREDDIE CAME A FEW MONTHS LATER...
AND A BETTER OFFER WAS MADE.
OF COURSE, THE MAN WHO BROUGHT ON THE TRUMPED-UP PACK OF LIES BEFORE –
WOULD MAKE MORE MOVES TO CHANGE THE CONTRACT...
EVEN TAKING A SHOT AT RANDY'S PARENTS –
YOU GUYS GO PICK IT UP FOR ME...
...BUT IT DIDN'T WORK.
MA PUT HER FOOT DOWN.
WE'RE NOT CHANGING A THING, FREDDIE!.. NOT A THING!!..
FASCINATI
THE GOLDEN BOY WAS COMING HOME TO CLAIM HIS PRIZE... WHAT HE WAS DESTINED TO DO –
BUT BE CAREFUL!
THE ACQUISITION OF THE VERY MACHINES HE GREW UP WITH...
THE VERY MACHINES HE AND HIS FAMILY LOVED.
– SIGN IT AND LET'S GET OUT OF HERE, ROC!..

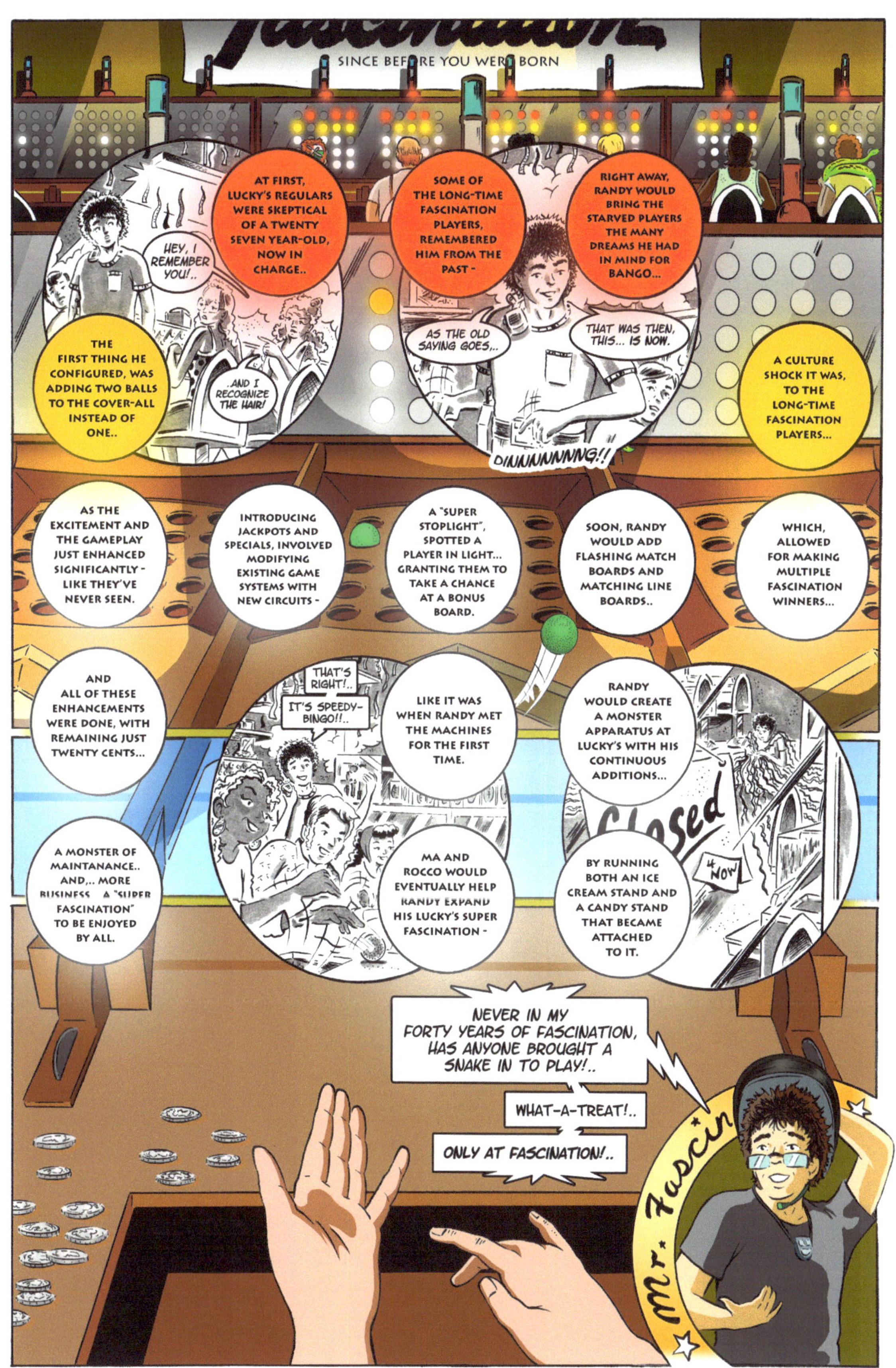
SINCE BEFORE YOU WERE BORN

AT FIRST, LUCKY'S REGULARS WERE SKEPTICAL OF A TWENTY SEVEN YEAR-OLD, NOW IN CHARGE..

SOME OF THE LONG-TIME FASCINATION PLAYERS, REMEMBERED HIM FROM THE PAST -

RIGHT AWAY, RANDY WOULD BRING THE STARVED PLAYERS THE MANY DREAMS HE HAD IN MIND FOR BANGO...

HEY, I REMEMBER YOU!..

..AND I RECOGNIZE THE HAIR!

AS THE OLD SAYING GOES...

THAT WAS THEN, THIS... IS NOW.

THE FIRST THING HE CONFIGURED, WAS ADDING TWO BALLS TO THE COVER-ALL INSTEAD OF ONE..

A CULTURE SHOCK IT WAS, TO THE LONG-TIME FASCINATION PLAYERS...

DINNNNNNNG!!

AS THE EXCITEMENT AND THE GAMEPLAY JUST ENHANCED SIGNIFICANTLY - LIKE THEY'VE NEVER SEEN.

INTRODUCING JACKPOTS AND SPECIALS, INVOLVED MODIFYING EXISTING GAME SYSTEMS WITH NEW CIRCUITS -

A "SUPER STOPLIGHT", SPOTTED A PLAYER IN LIGHT... GRANTING THEM TO TAKE A CHANCE AT A BONUS BOARD.

SOON, RANDY WOULD ADD FLASHING MATCH BOARDS AND MATCHING LINE BOARDS..

WHICH, ALLOWED FOR MAKING MULTIPLE FASCINATION WINNERS...

AND ALL OF THESE ENHANCEMENTS WERE DONE, WITH REMAINING JUST TWENTY CENTS...

THAT'S RIGHT!..

IT'S SPEEDY-BINGO!!..

LIKE IT WAS WHEN RANDY MET THE MACHINES FOR THE FIRST TIME.

RANDY WOULD CREATE A MONSTER APPARATUS AT LUCKY'S WITH HIS CONTINUOUS ADDITIONS...

Closed 4 NOW

A MONSTER OF MAINTANANCE.. AND,.. MORE BUSINESS. A "SUPER FASCINATION" TO BE ENJOYED BY ALL.

MA AND ROCCO WOULD EVENTUALLY HELP RANDY EXPAND HIS LUCKY'S SUPER FASCINATION -

BY RUNNING BOTH AN ICE CREAM STAND AND A CANDY STAND THAT BECAME ATTACHED TO IT.

NEVER IN MY FORTY YEARS OF FASCINATION, HAS ANYONE BROUGHT A SNAKE IN TO PLAY!..

WHAT-A-TREAT!..

ONLY AT FASCINATION!..

Mr. Fascin

DINNNNNNG!!
THE BELT
SINCE BEFORE YOU WERE BORN
HAHA - YEAH, I WON AGAIN!
THE REBIRTH OF LUCKY'S
ALRIGHT, THE YOUNG MAN ON THE TOP ROW HAS TAKEN THAT SPEEDY BINGO ROUND!..
CAN HE.. WILL HE?.. DO IT AGAIN?!..
Mr. Fascination

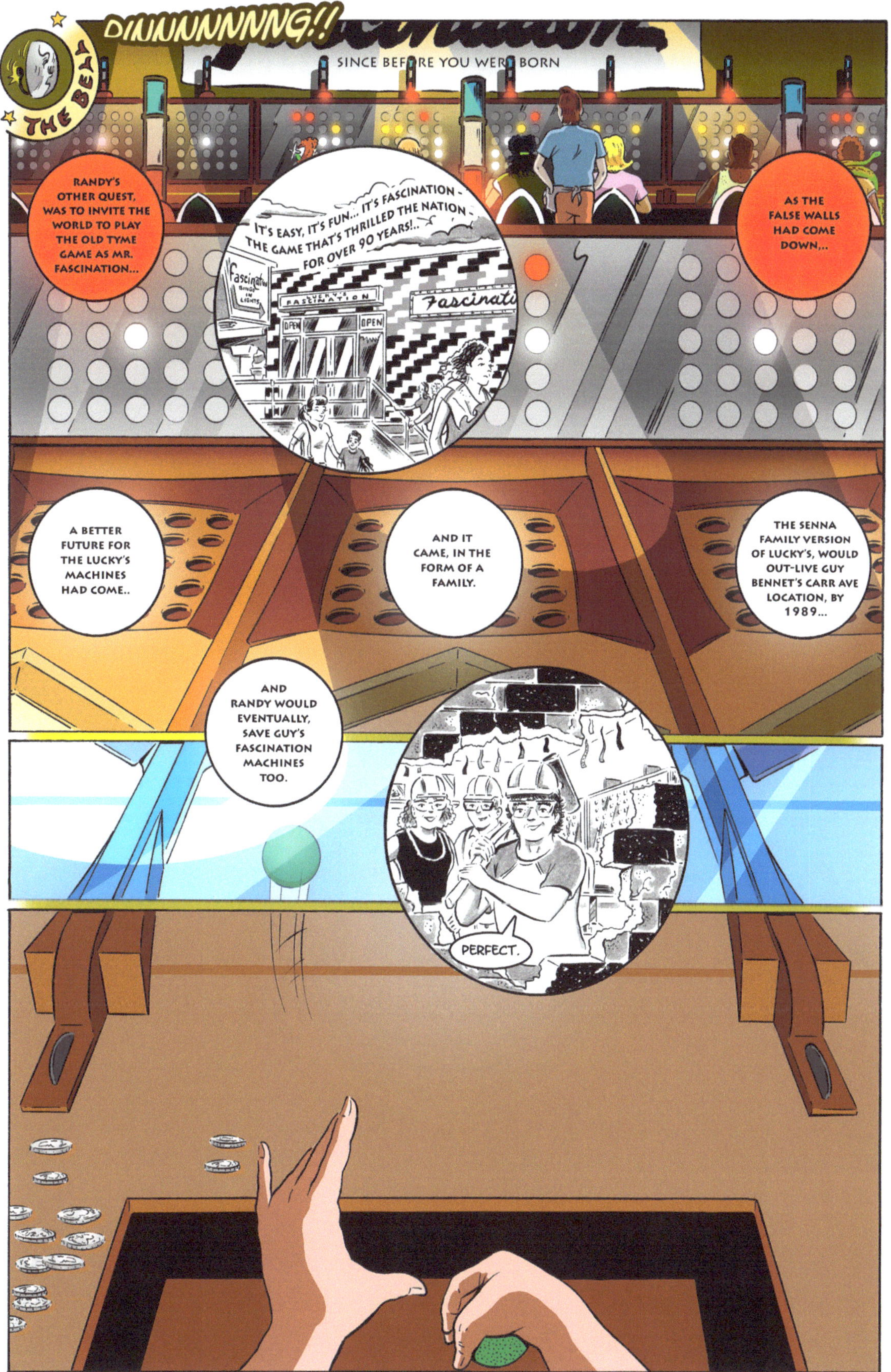

THE BEAT
DINNNNNNNG!!
SINCE BEFORE YOU WERE BORN
RANDY'S OTHER QUEST, WAS TO INVITE THE WORLD TO PLAY THE OLD TYME GAME AS MR. FASCINATION...
IT'S EASY, IT'S FUN... IT'S FASCINATION - THE GAME THAT'S THRILLED THE NATION FOR OVER 90 YEARS!...
AS THE FALSE WALLS HAD COME DOWN,...
A BETTER FUTURE FOR THE LUCKY'S MACHINES HAD COME..
AND IT CAME, IN THE FORM OF A FAMILY.
THE SENNA FAMILY VERSION OF LUCKY'S, WOULD OUT-LIVE GUY BENNET'S CARR AVE LOCATION, BY 1989...
AND RANDY WOULD EVENTUALLY, SAVE GUY'S FASCINATION MACHINES TOO.
PERFECT.

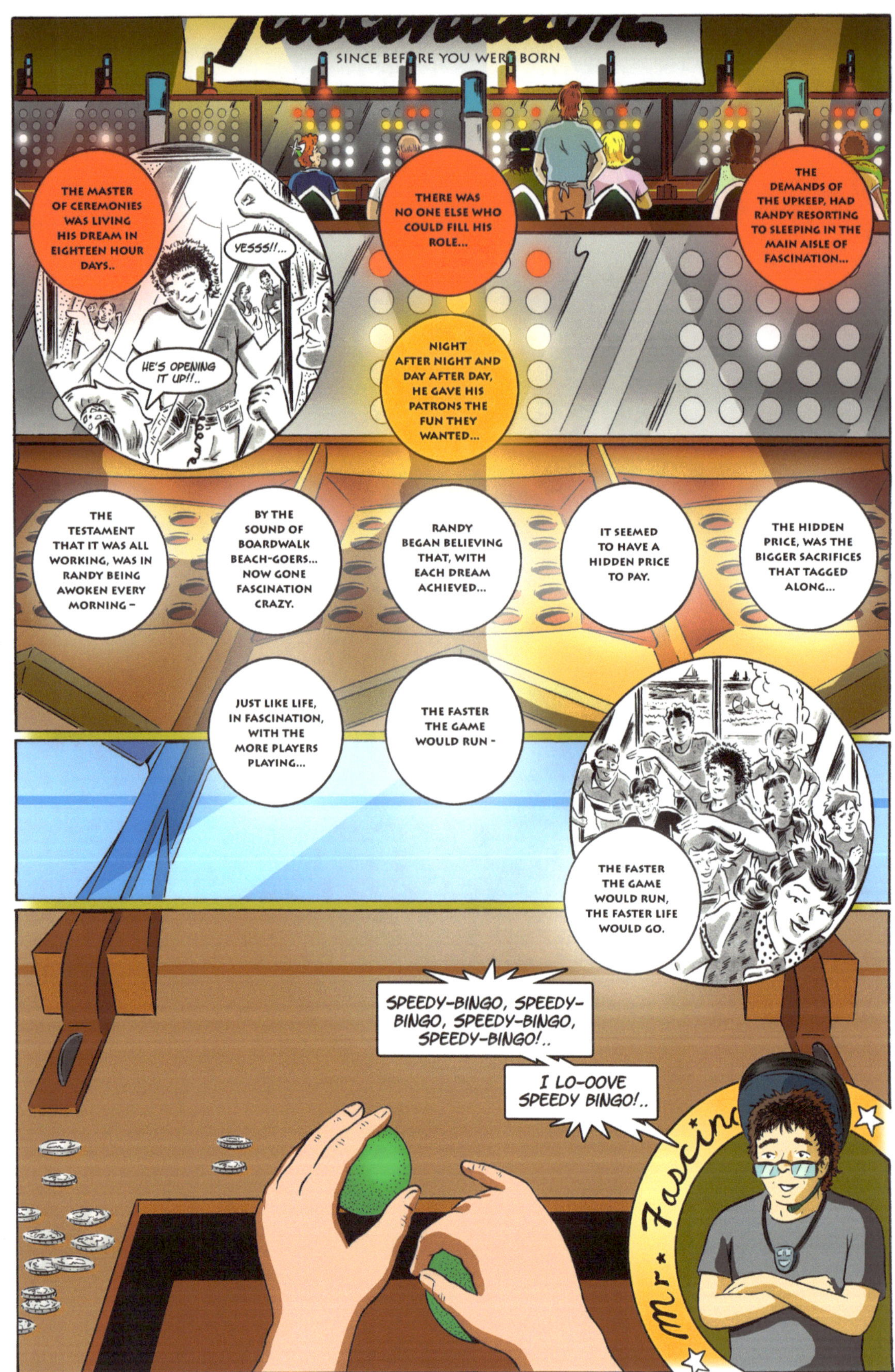
SINCE BEFORE YOU WERE BORN
THE MASTER OF CEREMONIES WAS LIVING HIS DREAM IN EIGHTEEN HOUR DAYS..
YESSS!!...
HE'S OPENING IT UP!!..
THERE WAS NO ONE ELSE WHO COULD FILL HIS ROLE...
THE DEMANDS OF THE UPKEEP, HAD RANDY RESORTING TO SLEEPING IN THE MAIN AISLE OF FASCINATION...
NIGHT AFTER NIGHT AND DAY AFTER DAY, HE GAVE HIS PATRONS THE FUN THEY WANTED...
THE TESTAMENT THAT IT WAS ALL WORKING, WAS IN RANDY BEING AWOKEN EVERY MORNING –
BY THE SOUND OF BOARDWALK BEACH-GOERS... NOW GONE FASCINATION CRAZY.
RANDY BEGAN BELIEVING THAT, WITH EACH DREAM ACHIEVED...
IT SEEMED TO HAVE A HIDDEN PRICE TO PAY.
THE HIDDEN PRICE, WAS THE BIGGER SACRIFICES THAT TAGGED ALONG...
JUST LIKE LIFE, IN FASCINATION, WITH THE MORE PLAYERS PLAYING...
THE FASTER THE GAME WOULD RUN –
THE FASTER THE GAME WOULD RUN, THE FASTER LIFE WOULD GO.
SPEEDY-BINGO, SPEEDY-BINGO, SPEEDY-BINGO, SPEEDY-BINGO!..
I LO-OOVE SPEEDY BINGO!..
Mr. Fascina

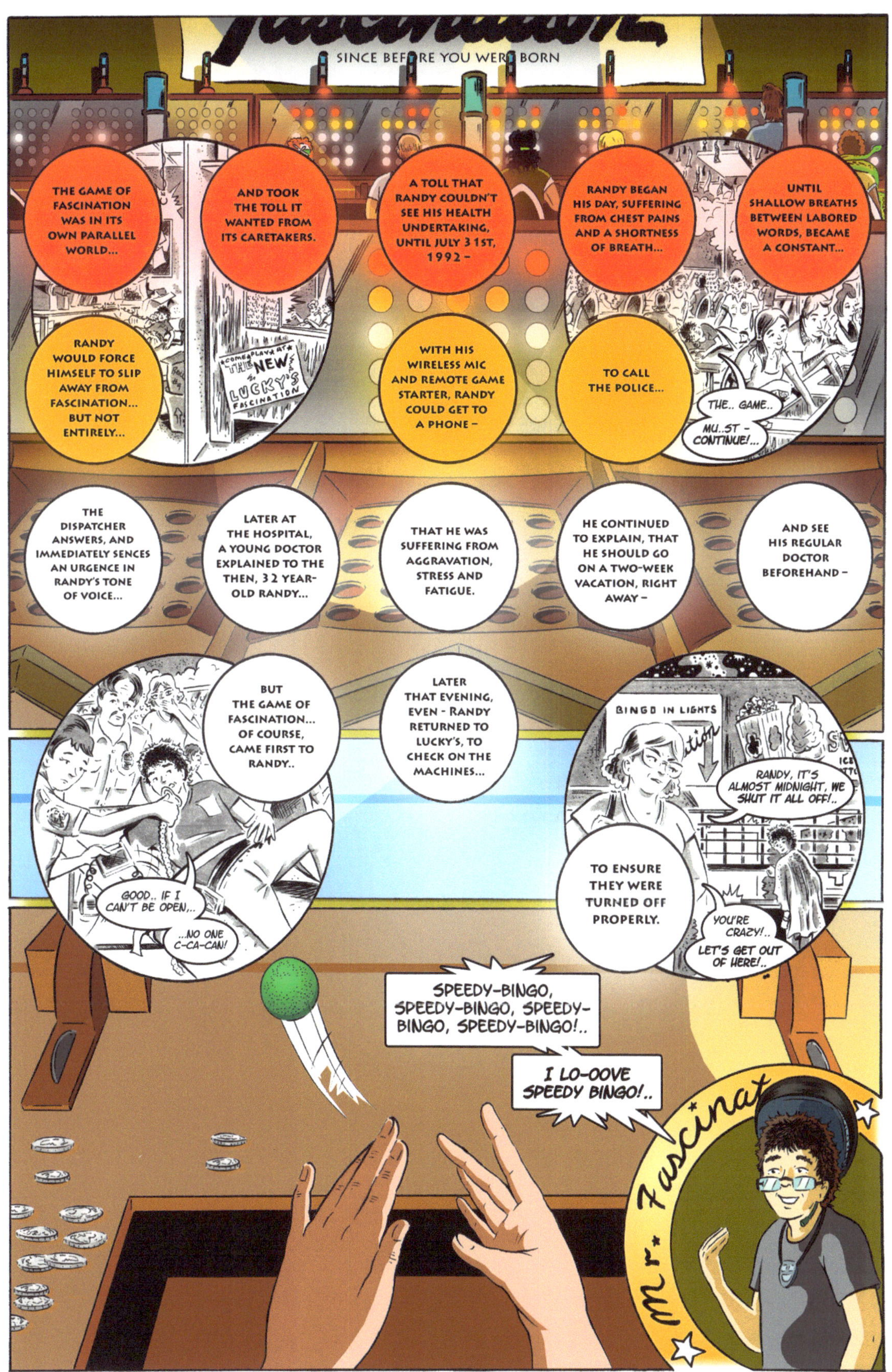
SINCE BEFORE YOU WERE BORN
THE GAME OF FASCINATION WAS IN ITS OWN PARALLEL WORLD...
AND TOOK THE TOLL IT WANTED FROM ITS CARETAKERS.
A TOLL THAT RANDY COULDN'T SEE HIS HEALTH UNDERTAKING, UNTIL JULY 31ST, 1992 –
RANDY BEGAN HIS DAY, SUFFERING FROM CHEST PAINS AND A SHORTNESS OF BREATH...
UNTIL SHALLOW BREATHS BETWEEN LABORED WORDS, BECAME A CONSTANT...
RANDY WOULD FORCE HIMSELF TO SLIP AWAY FROM FASCINATION... BUT NOT ENTIRELY...
COME PLAY AT THE NEW LUCKY'S FASCINATION
WITH HIS WIRELESS MIC AND REMOTE GAME STARTER, RANDY COULD GET TO A PHONE –
TO CALL THE POLICE...
THE.. GAME.. MU..ST – CONTINUE!...
THE DISPATCHER ANSWERS, AND IMMEDIATELY SENCES AN URGENCE IN RANDY'S TONE OF VOICE...
LATER AT THE HOSPITAL, A YOUNG DOCTOR EXPLAINED TO THE THEN, 32 YEAR-OLD RANDY...
THAT HE WAS SUFFERING FROM AGGRAVATION, STRESS AND FATIGUE.
HE CONTINUED TO EXPLAIN, THAT HE SHOULD GO ON A TWO-WEEK VACATION, RIGHT AWAY –
AND SEE HIS REGULAR DOCTOR BEFOREHAND –
BUT THE GAME OF FASCINATION... OF COURSE, CAME FIRST TO RANDY..
LATER THAT EVENING, EVEN - RANDY RETURNED TO LUCKY'S, TO CHECK ON THE MACHINES...
BINGO IN LIGHTS
RANDY, IT'S ALMOST MIDNIGHT, WE SHUT IT ALL OFF!..
GOOD.. IF I CAN'T BE OPEN,..
...NO ONE C-CA-CAN!
TO ENSURE THEY WERE TURNED OFF PROPERLY.
YOU'RE CRAZY!.. LET'S GET OUT OF HERE!..
SPEEDY-BINGO, SPEEDY-BINGO, SPEEDY-BINGO, SPEEDY-BINGO!..
I LO-OOVE SPEEDY BINGO!..
Mr. Fascinat

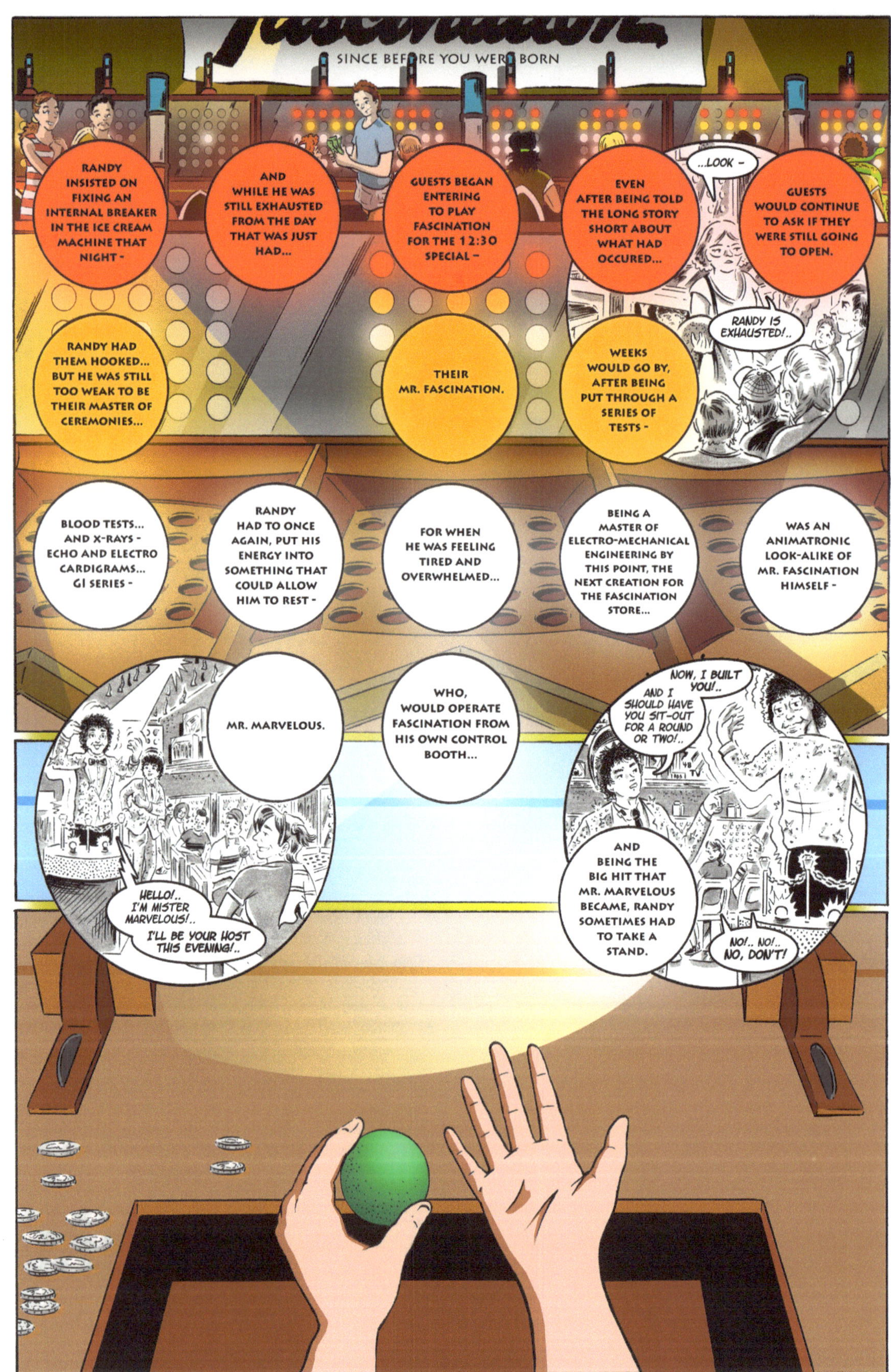
SINCE BEFORE YOU WERE BORN

RANDY INSISTED ON FIXING AN INTERNAL BREAKER IN THE ICE CREAM MACHINE THAT NIGHT -

AND WHILE HE WAS STILL EXHAUSTED FROM THE DAY THAT WAS JUST HAD...

GUESTS BEGAN ENTERING TO PLAY FASCINATION FOR THE 12:30 SPECIAL -

EVEN AFTER BEING TOLD THE LONG STORY SHORT ABOUT WHAT HAD OCCURED...

...LOOK -

RANDY IS EXHAUSTED!..

GUESTS WOULD CONTINUE TO ASK IF THEY WERE STILL GOING TO OPEN.

RANDY HAD THEM HOOKED... BUT HE WAS STILL TOO WEAK TO BE THEIR MASTER OF CEREMONIES...

THEIR MR. FASCINATION.

WEEKS WOULD GO BY, AFTER BEING PUT THROUGH A SERIES OF TESTS -

BLOOD TESTS... AND X-RAYS - ECHO AND ELECTRO CARDIGRAMS... GI SERIES -

RANDY HAD TO ONCE AGAIN, PUT HIS ENERGY INTO SOMETHING THAT COULD ALLOW HIM TO REST -

FOR WHEN HE WAS FEELING TIRED AND OVERWHELMED...

BEING A MASTER OF ELECTRO-MECHANICAL ENGINEERING BY THIS POINT, THE NEXT CREATION FOR THE FASCINATION STORE...

WAS AN ANIMATRONIC LOOK-ALIKE OF MR. FASCINATION HIMSELF -

MR. MARVELOUS.

WHO, WOULD OPERATE FASCINATION FROM HIS OWN CONTROL BOOTH...

NOW, I BUILT YOU!.. AND I SHOULD HAVE YOU SIT-OUT FOR A ROUND OR TWO!..

HELLO!.. I'M MISTER MARVELOUS!..

I'LL BE YOUR HOST THIS EVENING!..

AND BEING THE BIG HIT THAT MR. MARVELOUS BECAME, RANDY SOMETIMES HAD TO TAKE A STAND.

NO!.. NO!.. NO, DON'T!

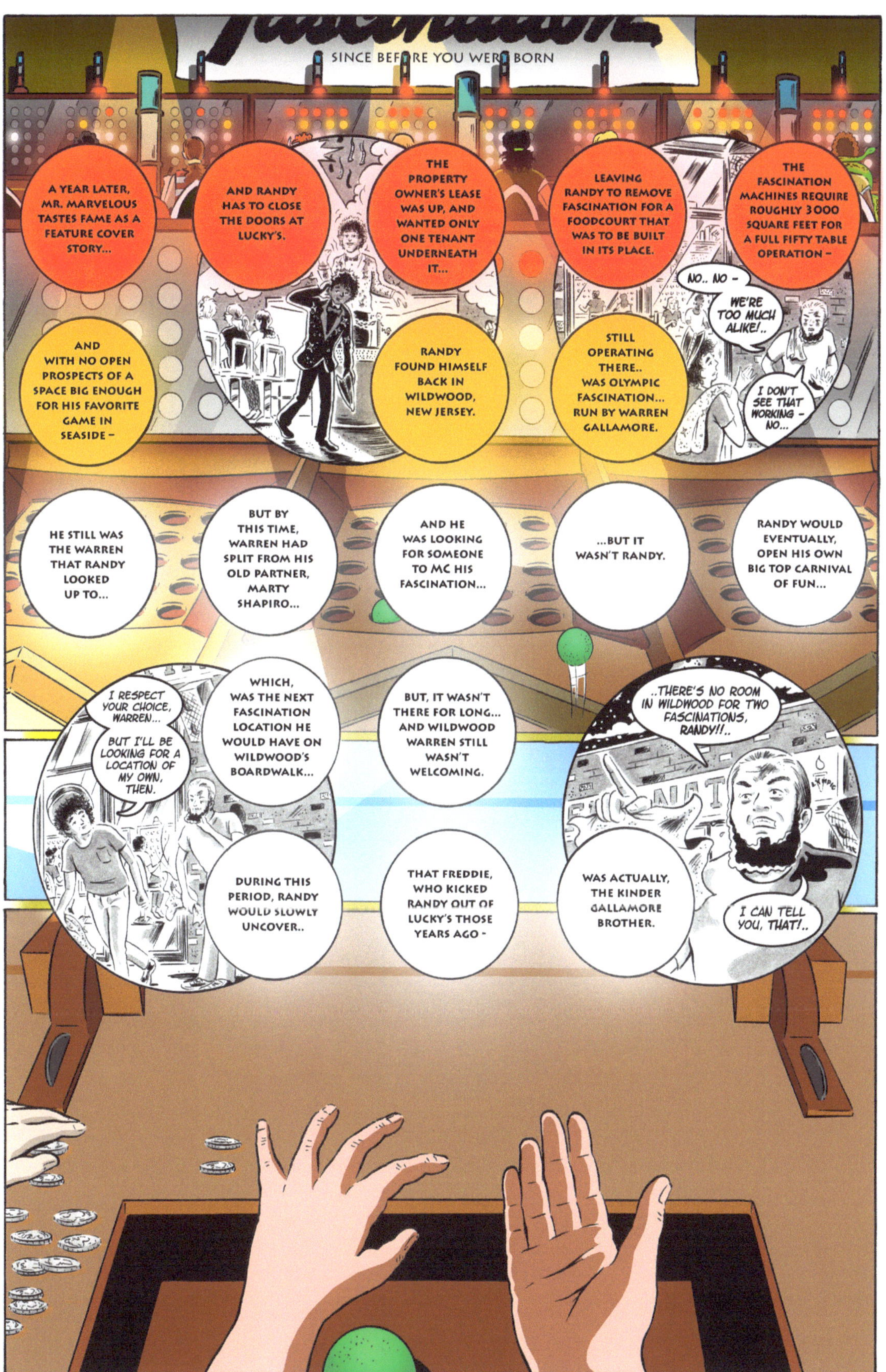
FASCINATION
SINCE BEFORE YOU WERE BORN

A YEAR LATER, MR. MARVELOUS TASTES FAME AS A FEATURE COVER STORY...

AND RANDY HAS TO CLOSE THE DOORS AT LUCKY'S.

THE PROPERTY OWNER'S LEASE WAS UP, AND WANTED ONLY ONE TENANT UNDERNEATH IT...

LEAVING RANDY TO REMOVE FASCINATION FOR A FOODCOURT THAT WAS TO BE BUILT IN ITS PLACE.

THE FASCINATION MACHINES REQUIRE ROUGHLY 3000 SQUARE FEET FOR A FULL FIFTY TABLE OPERATION –

NO.. NO –

WE'RE TOO MUCH ALIKE!..

I DON'T SEE THAT WORKING – NO...

AND WITH NO OPEN PROSPECTS OF A SPACE BIG ENOUGH FOR HIS FAVORITE GAME IN SEASIDE –

RANDY FOUND HIMSELF BACK IN WILDWOOD, NEW JERSEY.

STILL OPERATING THERE.. WAS OLYMPIC FASCINATION... RUN BY WARREN GALLAMORE.

HE STILL WAS THE WARREN THAT RANDY LOOKED UP TO...

BUT BY THIS TIME, WARREN HAD SPLIT FROM HIS OLD PARTNER, MARTY SHAPIRO...

AND HE WAS LOOKING FOR SOMEONE TO MC HIS FASCINATION...

...BUT IT WASN'T RANDY.

RANDY WOULD EVENTUALLY, OPEN HIS OWN BIG TOP CARNIVAL OF FUN...

I RESPECT YOUR CHOICE, WARREN...

BUT I'LL BE LOOKING FOR A LOCATION OF MY OWN, THEN.

WHICH, WAS THE NEXT FASCINATION LOCATION HE WOULD HAVE ON WILDWOOD'S BOARDWALK...

BUT, IT WASN'T THERE FOR LONG... AND WILDWOOD WARREN STILL WASN'T WELCOMING.

..THERE'S NO ROOM IN WILDWOOD FOR TWO FASCINATIONS, RANDY!!..

DURING THIS PERIOD, RANDY WOULD SLOWLY UNCOVER..

THAT FREDDIE, WHO KICKED RANDY OUT OF LUCKY'S THOSE YEARS AGO –

WAS ACTUALLY, THE KINDER GALLAMORE BROTHER.

I CAN TELL YOU, THAT!..

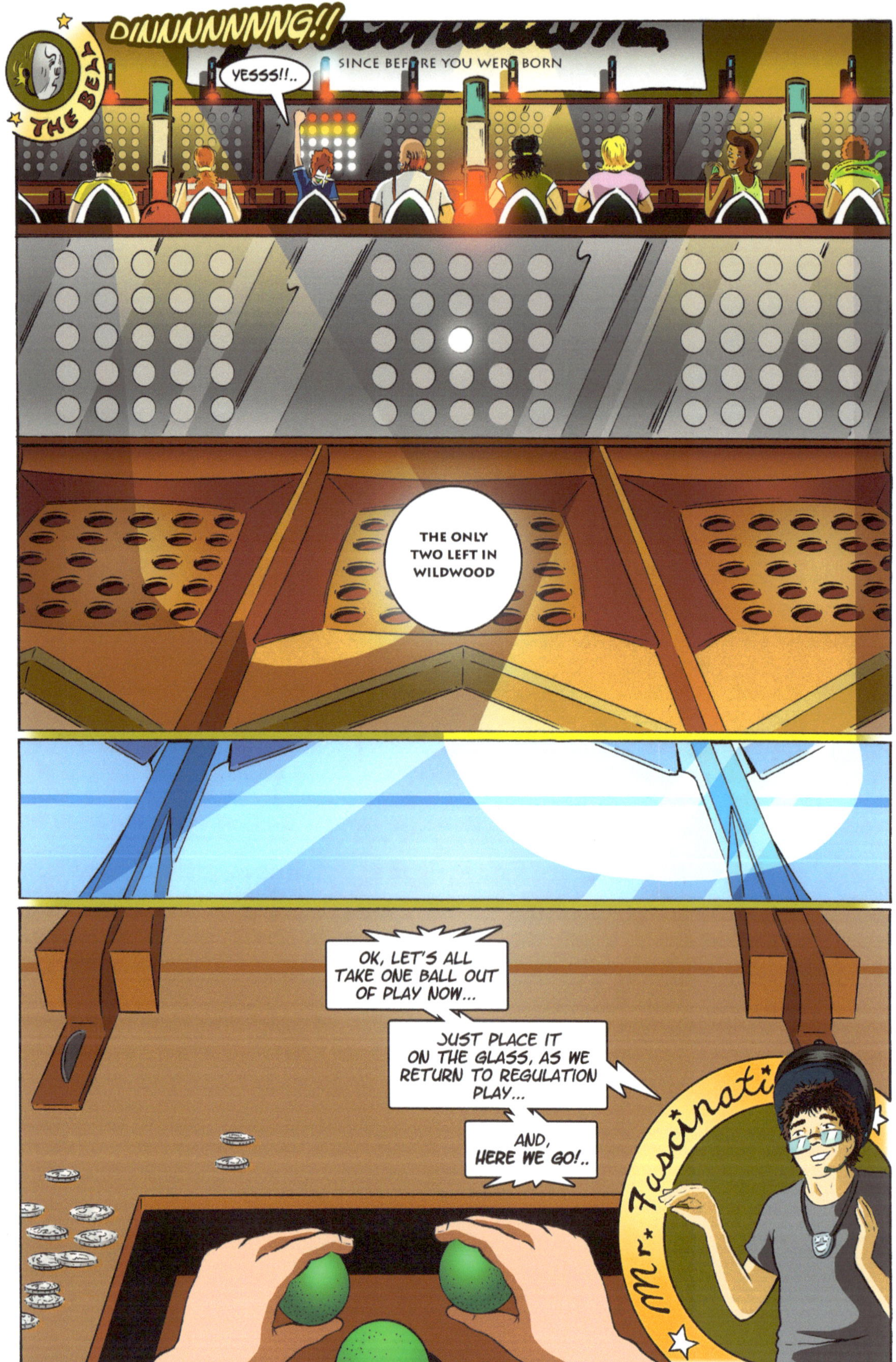

DINNNNNNNG!!
THE BELL
SINCE BEFORE YOU WERE BORN
YESSS!!..
THE ONLY TWO LEFT IN WILDWOOD
OK, LET'S ALL TAKE ONE BALL OUT OF PLAY NOW...
JUST PLACE IT ON THE GLASS, AS WE RETURN TO REGULATION PLAY...
AND, HERE WE GO!..
Mr. Fascinati

DINNNNNNNG!!
SINCE BEFORE YOU WERE BORN
THE BELT
DURING THE FIRST FIVE MONTHS OF THE BIG TOP CARNIVAL OF FUN'S EXISTANCE...
MAIN ENTRANCE
CARNIVAL
MULTI-LEVEL
ARCADE MUSEUM
ENTER HERE
WARREN WOULD START HIS CAMPAIGN OF SLANDER –
OVER HIS LOUD SPEAKERS, HE WOULD SPEAK ILL OF RANDY –
AND RANDY WOULD GET WORD OF THE SLANDER, FROM PLAYERS WHO PLAYED AT BOTH FASCINATION LOCATIONS –
WHAT THEY DIDN'T KNOW, WAS THAT WARREN WAS ONCE CONSIDERED A MENTOR TO RANDY...
TO ATTACK HIM IN THE PUBLIC, WITHIN HIS COMPLEX OF AMUSEMENTS...
N
OLYMPIC
WE'VE GOT A NEW FASCINATION IN WILDWOOD, FOLKS!.. – TOO BAD HE'S A CROOK!..
WAS REALLY DISTURBING TO RANDY...
THE MAN WHO LOOKS LIKE ABE LINCOLN?.. HE SAYS THINGS ABOUT YOU..
DON'T GO DOWN THE BOARDWALK –
FLIPPER'S WON'T REDEEM YOUR COUPONS, FOLKS!..
USE OF LIGHTS
AND IT DISTURBED BOTH OF THEIR CUSTOMERS... AT BOTH ENDS OF THE BOARDWALK.
ALMOST TO NO END.
...HERE WE GO – ROLLING FOR FIVE IN A ROW, NOW – ANY DIRECTION!...
UP AND DOWN, SIDE TO SIDE, CORNER TO CORNER!..
Mr. Fascina

SINCE BEFORE YOU WERE BORN
FASCINATION'S ROUGHLY UNKEMPT PAST, KEPT LURKING -
RANDY WOULD UNDERGO A LAWSUIT WITH THE BIG TOP CARNIVAL LOCATION'S LANDLORD...
AS THE BUILDING PROVED TO BE FAULTY DURING HIS OCCUPANCY...
AFTER SOME STORMS, THE CEILING GAVE WAY... DAMAGING THE LUCKY'S FASCINATION MACHINES.
THE BIGGER ISSUE... WAS DISRUPTING THE SENNA FAMILY BUSINESS.
SO MUCH MONEY WAS SPENT ON THE LAWSUIT, THE SENNA'S LOST THEIR HOME IN MIDDLETOWN.
THE MACHINES WOULD RETURN TO STORAGE, AND RANDY WOULD TAKE 1996 ON INSTEAD -
FUN
MAIN ENTRANCE
CAT
WITH DEVELPING PATENTS. PATENTS FOR TWO GAMES RANDY WOULD DEVELOP FOR THE I.A.A.P.A. -
THE INTERNATIONAL ASSOCIATION OF AMUSEMENT PARKS AND ATTRACTIONS TRADESHOW.
HOUSE FOR SALE BY OWNER
"THE MEN'S ROOM" WAS A SENSATION AT THE SHOW AND WAS AWARDED FIRST PLACE.
MEN'S ROOM
FLASH!
FLASH!
DO YOU HAVE EXPERIENCE IN AMUSEMENTS?..
EXPERIENCE?..
HOW'S A LIFETIME??..

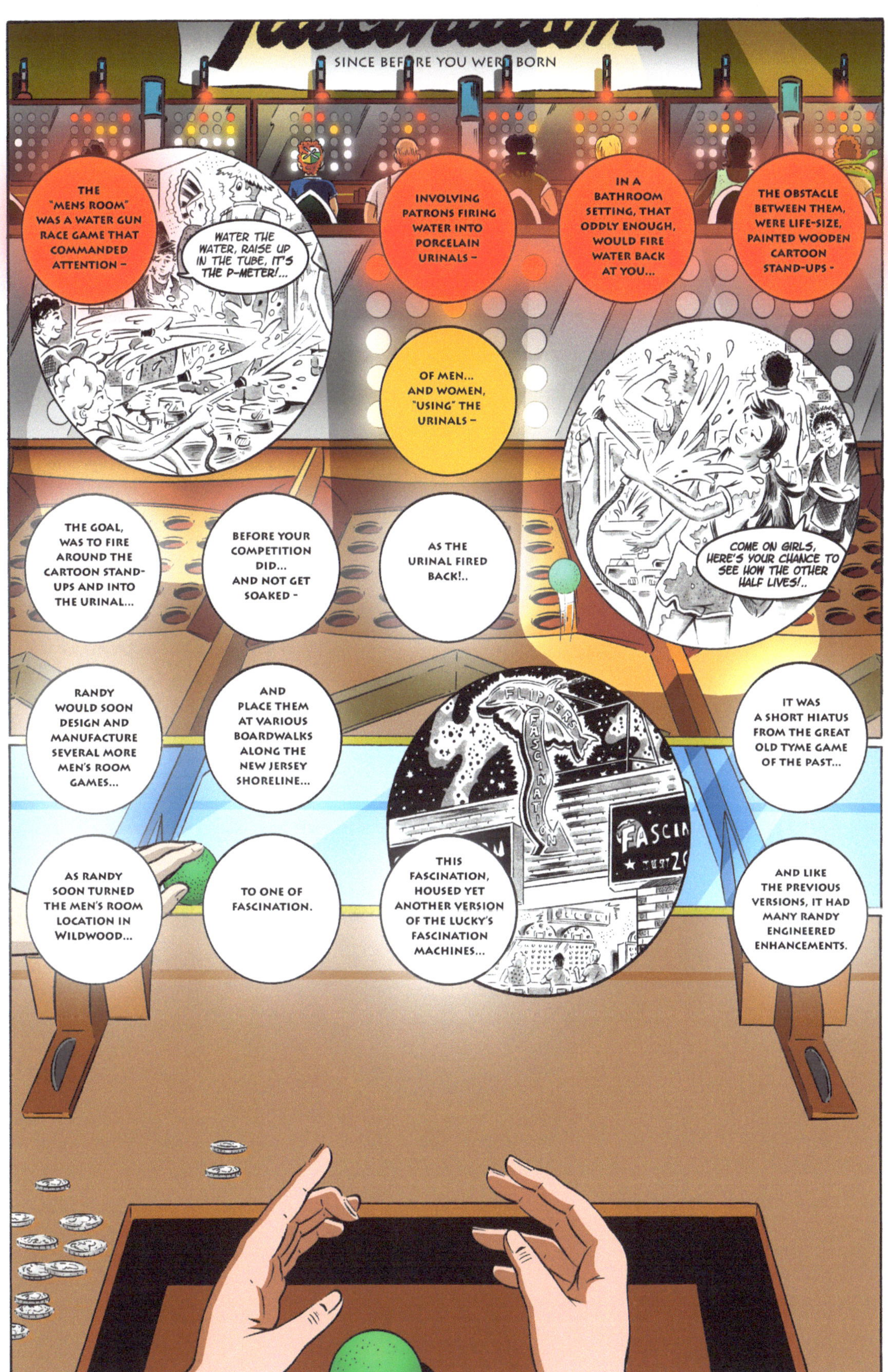

SINCE BEFORE YOU WERE BORN
THE "MENS ROOM" WAS A WATER GUN RACE GAME THAT COMMANDED ATTENTION –
WATER THE WATER, RAISE UP IN THE TUBE, IT'S THE P-METER!...
INVOLVING PATRONS FIRING WATER INTO PORCELAIN URINALS –
IN A BATHROOM SETTING, THAT ODDLY ENOUGH, WOULD FIRE WATER BACK AT YOU...
THE OBSTACLE BETWEEN THEM, WERE LIFE-SIZE, PAINTED WOODEN CARTOON STAND-UPS –
OF MEN... AND WOMEN, "USING" THE URINALS –
THE GOAL, WAS TO FIRE AROUND THE CARTOON STAND-UPS AND INTO THE URINAL...
BEFORE YOUR COMPETITION DID... AND NOT GET SOAKED –
AS THE URINAL FIRED BACK!..
COME ON GIRLS, HERE'S YOUR CHANCE TO SEE HOW THE OTHER HALF LIVES!..
RANDY WOULD SOON DESIGN AND MANUFACTURE SEVERAL MORE MEN'S ROOM GAMES...
AND PLACE THEM AT VARIOUS BOARDWALKS ALONG THE NEW JERSEY SHORELINE...
IT WAS A SHORT HIATUS FROM THE GREAT OLD TYME GAME OF THE PAST...
AS RANDY SOON TURNED THE MEN'S ROOM LOCATION IN WILDWOOD...
TO ONE OF FASCINATION.
THIS FASCINATION, HOUSED YET ANOTHER VERSION OF THE LUCKY'S FASCINATION MACHINES...
AND LIKE THE PREVIOUS VERSIONS, IT HAD MANY RANDY ENGINEERED ENHANCEMENTS.
FLIPPERS
FASCINATION
FASCIN

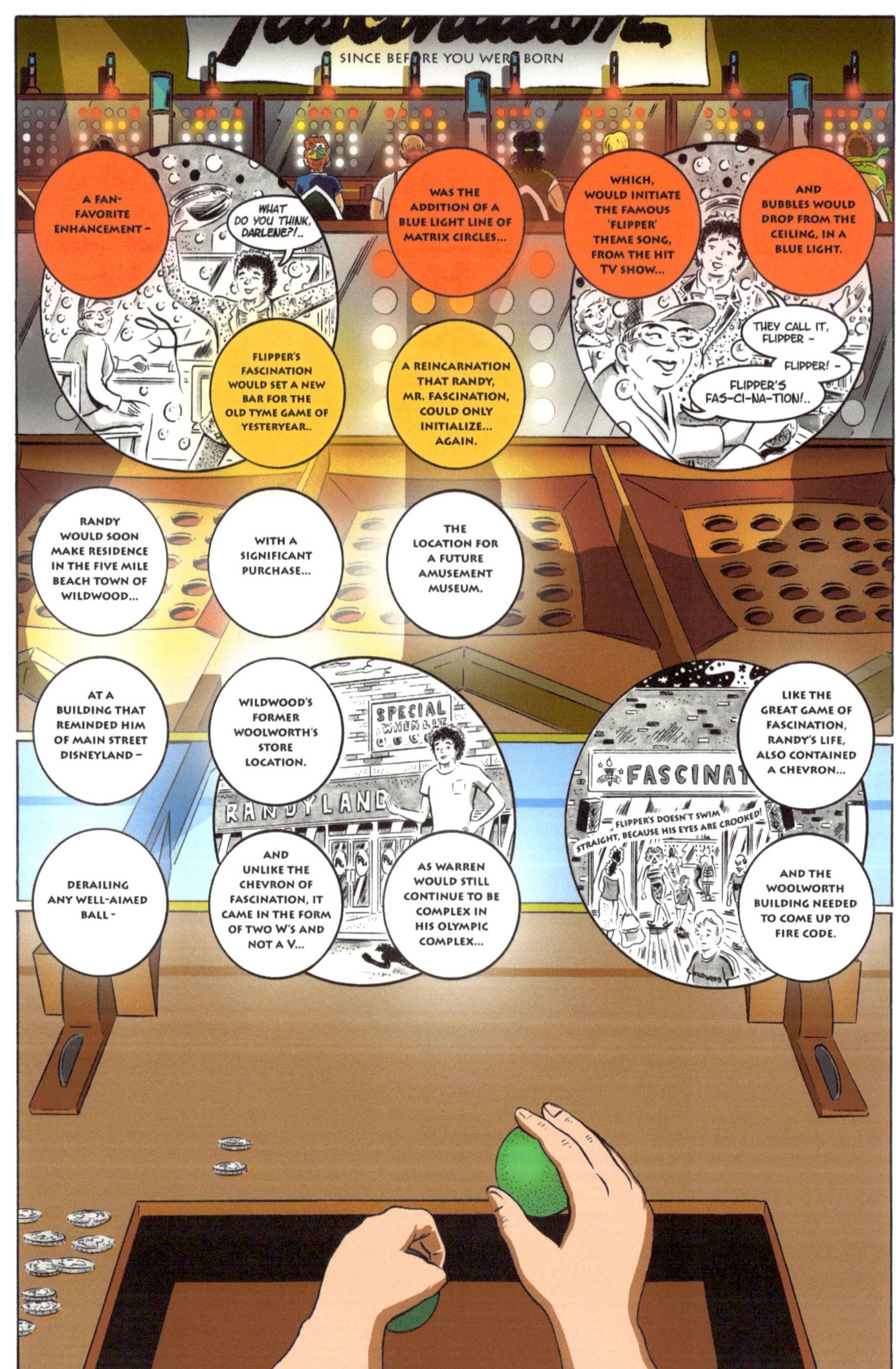

SINCE BEFORE YOU WERE BORN

A FAN-FAVORITE ENHANCEMENT –

WHAT DO YOU THINK, DARLENE?!..

WAS THE ADDITION OF A BLUE LIGHT LINE OF MATRIX CIRCLES...

WHICH, WOULD INITIATE THE FAMOUS 'FLIPPER' THEME SONG, FROM THE HIT TV SHOW...

AND BUBBLES WOULD DROP FROM THE CEILING, IN A BLUE LIGHT.

FLIPPER'S FASCINATION WOULD SET A NEW BAR FOR THE OLD TYME GAME OF YESTERYEAR..

A REINCARNATION THAT RANDY, MR. FASCINATION, COULD ONLY INITIALIZE... AGAIN.

THEY CALL IT, FLIPPER –

FLIPPER! –

FLIPPER'S FAS-CI-NA-TION!..

RANDY WOULD SOON MAKE RESIDENCE IN THE FIVE MILE BEACH TOWN OF WILDWOOD...

WITH A SIGNIFICANT PURCHASE...

THE LOCATION FOR A FUTURE AMUSEMENT MUSEUM.

AT A BUILDING THAT REMINDED HIM OF MAIN STREET DISNEYLAND –

WILDWOOD'S FORMER WOOLWORTH'S STORE LOCATION.

SPECIAL WHEN LIT

RANDYLAND

FASCINAT

FLIPPER'S DOESN'T SWIM STRAIGHT, BECAUSE HIS EYES ARE CROOKED!

LIKE THE GREAT GAME OF FASCINATION, RANDY'S LIFE, ALSO CONTAINED A CHEVRON...

DERAILING ANY WELL-AIMED BALL –

AND UNLIKE THE CHEVRON OF FASCINATION, IT CAME IN THE FORM OF TWO W'S AND NOT A V...

AS WARREN WOULD STILL CONTINUE TO BE COMPLEX IN HIS OLYMPIC COMPLEX...

AND THE WOOLWORTH BUILDING NEEDED TO COME UP TO FIRE CODE.

DINNNNNNG!!
THE BEAT
SINCE BEFORE YOU WERE BORN
ALRIGHT, HONEY!..
- WOO-HOO!
THE
W-SHAPED
CHEVRON
AND WE HAVE ANOTHER WINNER!..
LOOK AT YOU!.. WITH JUST SIX LEFT ON THE STOP LIGHT!..
LET'S PLAY ANOTHER, - HERE WE GO!..
Mr. Fascina

55

DINNNNNNNG!!
THE BEST
SINCE BEFORE YOU WERE BORN
IT'S SEEN ON TV
NEVERMIND THE W-SHAPED CHEVRONS... I'LL GET AROUND BOTH –
WHAT?.. WHAT DID HE SAY?..
THIS INVOLVED PARTNERING WITH A LOS ANGELES FILM PRODUCTION COMPANY...
RANDY WOULD THEN, PUT ENERGY INTO THE MUSEUM... FOR A POTENTIAL FUTURE OPENING..
HI-BALL
OVER HERE, WE HAVE...
EVEN MORE ELECTRO-MECHANICAL GAMES FROM DISNEYLAND AND WILDWOOD'S PAST...
TO CREATE A DOCUMENTARY ON FASCINATION – AND RANDY'S LIFE SPENT WITH IT...
BUT IT WAS NEVER RELEASED, DUE TO PRODUCTION DISAGREEMENTS...
DURING THE FILMING,.. SOME TRUTH CAME OUT FROM WARREN HIMSELF –
REVEALING, DEEP DOWN, THAT WARREN CONSIDERED RANDY AS SUPER-HUMAN.
WHAT CAN I SAY?..
THE GUY'S A GENIUS!..
AWK-AWK!
–EGHK!

fascination
SINCE BEFORE YOU WERE BORN
SOME MONTHS LATER, RANDY WAS ABLE TO OPEN IN WILDWOOD'S BOARDWALK MALL...
BOARDWALK MALL
RETRO ARCADE
OVER 25 UNIQUE STORES
THE MALL HOUSED ONE GIANT OPEN ROOM BELOW BOARDWALK LEVEL, WHICH COULD HOST THE FASCINATION MACHINES...
BUT IT WAS THE MACHINES THAT RANDY ACQUIRED FROM HERSHEY PENNSYLVANIA'S HERSHEY PARK...
AND FOR ANOTHER EIGHT YEARS, IT DID...
DINNNNNNNG!!
- AND WE HAVE A WINNER!..
PROPERTY OF HERSHEY PARK HERSHEY PA
ON THE DIAGNAL LINE - WAY TO GO!..
THAT WOULD OCCUPY THE ROOM WITH AN ARRAY OF RANDY'S OWN ELECTRO-MECHANICAL PINBALL MACHINES...
MOST OF WHICH, WERE FROM HIS CHILDHOOD AND OPERATING PERFECTLY.
AS RANDY WAS ALL ABOUT PRESERVATION...
PLAYABLE PRESERVATION.
AND AS THE NEXT CHAPTER OF LUCKY'S WAS BEGINNING TO FLOURISH AT THE BOARDWALK MALL -
- CAREFUL, NOW!..
THAT WAS MY FIRST.
BANG-BANG-BANG!
RANDY REALIZED HE TRIGGERED YET, ANOTHER THREAT TO WARREN'S EGO -
BUT IT PROVED TO BE TEMPORARY.
WARREN?!..

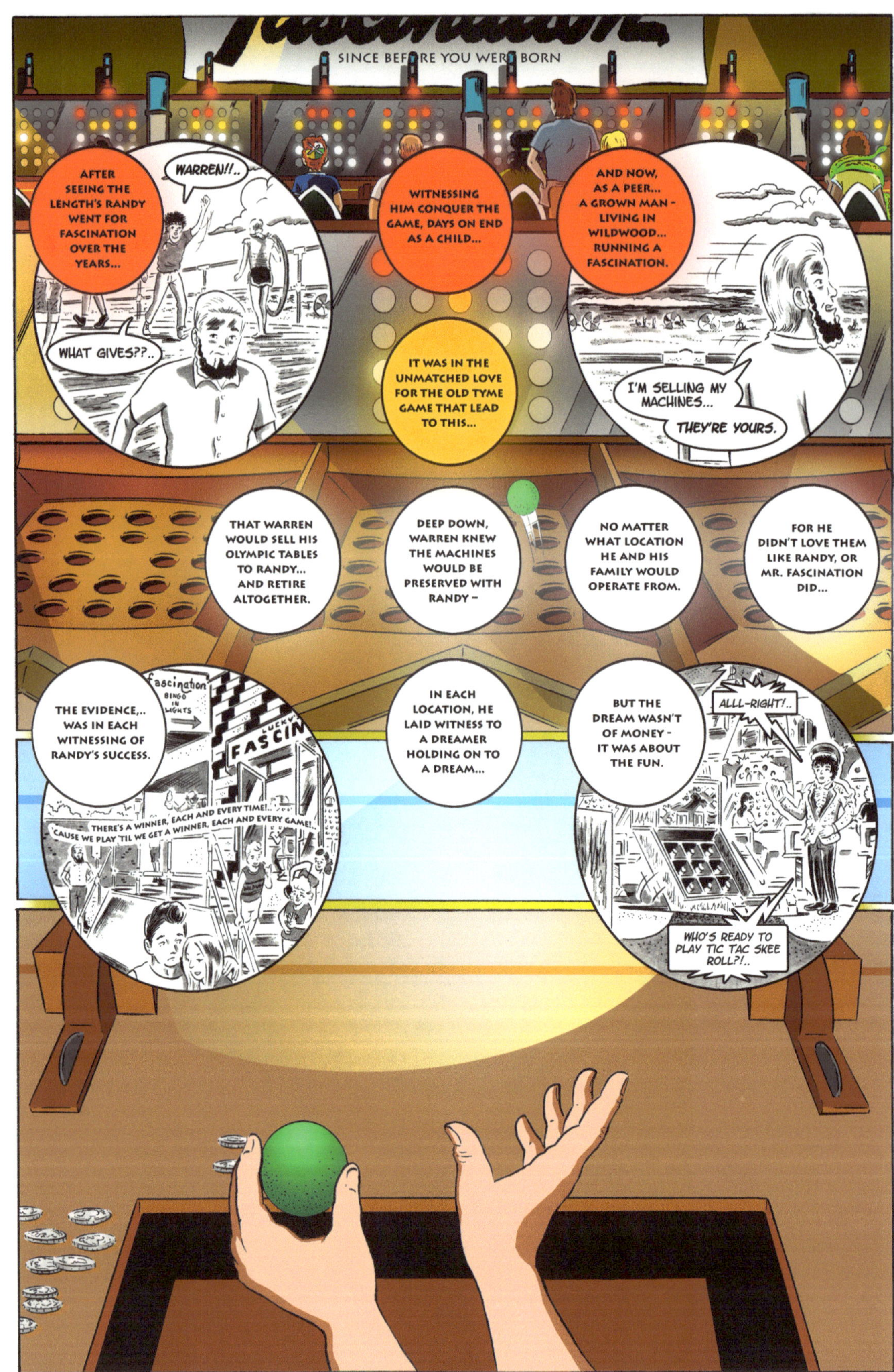
SINCE BEFORE YOU WERE BORN
AFTER SEEING THE LENGTH'S RANDY WENT FOR FASCINATION OVER THE YEARS...
WARREN!!..
WHAT GIVES??..
WITNESSING HIM CONQUER THE GAME, DAYS ON END AS A CHILD...
IT WAS IN THE UNMATCHED LOVE FOR THE OLD TYME GAME THAT LEAD TO THIS...
AND NOW, AS A PEER... A GROWN MAN - LIVING IN WILDWOOD... RUNNING A FASCINATION.
I'M SELLING MY MACHINES...
THEY'RE YOURS.
THAT WARREN WOULD SELL HIS OLYMPIC TABLES TO RANDY... AND RETIRE ALTOGETHER.
DEEP DOWN, WARREN KNEW THE MACHINES WOULD BE PRESERVED WITH RANDY –
NO MATTER WHAT LOCATION HE AND HIS FAMILY WOULD OPERATE FROM.
FOR HE DIDN'T LOVE THEM LIKE RANDY, OR MR. FASCINATION DID...
THE EVIDENCE,.. WAS IN EACH WITNESSING OF RANDY'S SUCCESS.
fascination BINGO IN LIGHTS
LUCKY FASCIN
THERE'S A WINNER, EACH AND EVERY TIME!.. 'CAUSE WE PLAY 'TIL WE GET A WINNER, EACH AND EVERY GAME!..
IN EACH LOCATION, HE LAID WITNESS TO A DREAMER HOLDING ON TO A DREAM...
BUT THE DREAM WASN'T OF MONEY - IT WAS ABOUT THE FUN.
ALLL-RIGHT!..
WHO'S READY TO PLAY TIC TAC SKEE ROLL?!..

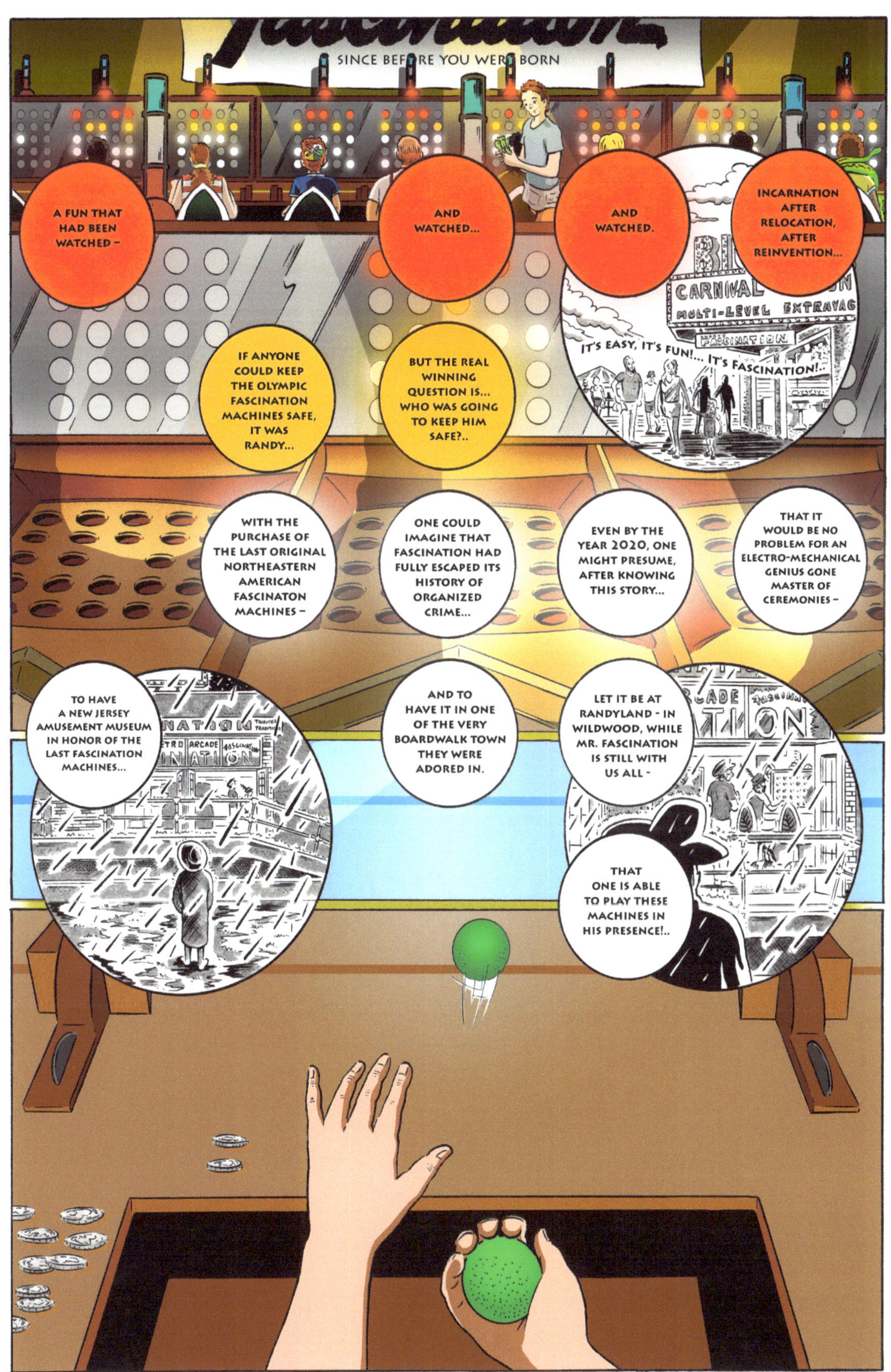

SINCE BEFORE YOU WERE BORN
A FUN THAT HAD BEEN WATCHED –
AND WATCHED...
AND WATCHED.
INCARNATION AFTER RELOCATION, AFTER REINVENTION...
IT'S EASY, IT'S FUN!... IT'S FASCINATION!..
BIG CARNIVAL
MULTI-LEVEL EXTRAVAG
FASCINATION
IF ANYONE COULD KEEP THE OLYMPIC FASCINATION MACHINES SAFE, IT WAS RANDY...
BUT THE REAL WINNING QUESTION IS... WHO WAS GOING TO KEEP HIM SAFE?..
WITH THE PURCHASE OF THE LAST ORIGINAL NORTHEASTERN AMERICAN FASCINATON MACHINES –
ONE COULD IMAGINE THAT FASCINATION HAD FULLY ESCAPED ITS HISTORY OF ORGANIZED CRIME...
EVEN BY THE YEAR 2020, ONE MIGHT PRESUME, AFTER KNOWING THIS STORY...
THAT IT WOULD BE NO PROBLEM FOR AN ELECTRO-MECHANICAL GENIUS GONE MASTER OF CEREMONIES –
TO HAVE A NEW JERSEY AMUSEMENT MUSEUM IN HONOR OF THE LAST FASCINATION MACHINES...
AND TO HAVE IT IN ONE OF THE VERY BOARDWALK TOWN THEY WERE ADORED IN.
LET IT BE AT RANDYLAND - IN WILDWOOD, WHILE MR. FASCINATION IS STILL WITH US ALL –
THAT ONE IS ABLE TO PLAY THESE MACHINES IN HIS PRESENCE!..

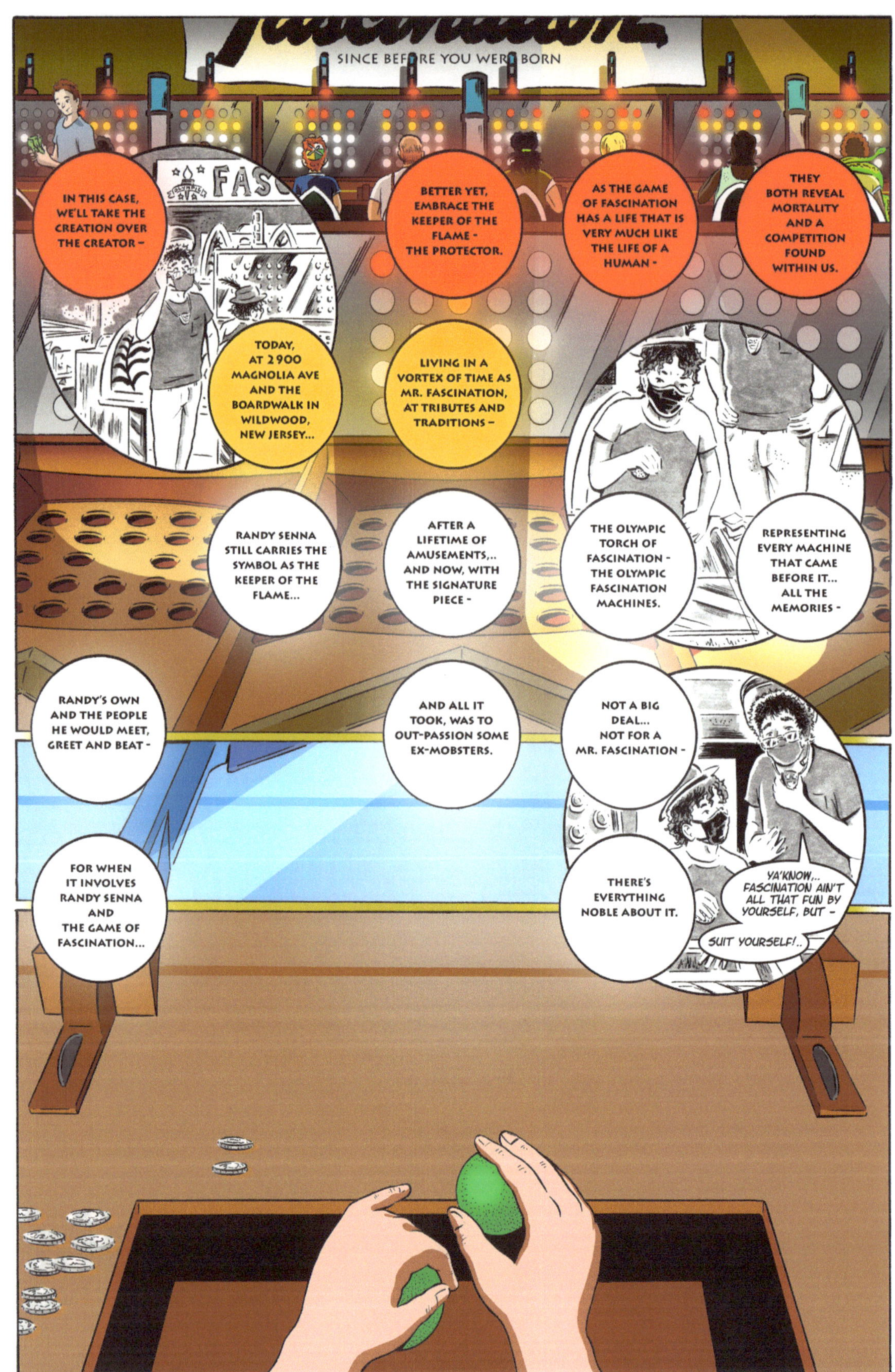
FASCINATION
SINCE BEFORE YOU WERE BORN
IN THIS CASE, WE'LL TAKE THE CREATION OVER THE CREATOR –
TODAY, AT 2900 MAGNOLIA AVE AND THE BOARDWALK IN WILDWOOD, NEW JERSEY...
BETTER YET, EMBRACE THE KEEPER OF THE FLAME – THE PROTECTOR.
LIVING IN A VORTEX OF TIME AS MR. FASCINATION, AT TRIBUTES AND TRADITIONS –
AS THE GAME OF FASCINATION HAS A LIFE THAT IS VERY MUCH LIKE THE LIFE OF A HUMAN –
THEY BOTH REVEAL MORTALITY AND A COMPETITION FOUND WITHIN US.
RANDY SENNA STILL CARRIES THE SYMBOL AS THE KEEPER OF THE FLAME...
AFTER A LIFETIME OF AMUSEMENTS,.. AND NOW, WITH THE SIGNATURE PIECE –
THE OLYMPIC TORCH OF FASCINATION – THE OLYMPIC FASCINATION MACHINES.
REPRESENTING EVERY MACHINE THAT CAME BEFORE IT... ALL THE MEMORIES –
RANDY'S OWN AND THE PEOPLE HE WOULD MEET, GREET AND BEAT –
AND ALL IT TOOK, WAS TO OUT-PASSION SOME EX-MOBSTERS.
NOT A BIG DEAL... NOT FOR A MR. FASCINATION –
FOR WHEN IT INVOLVES RANDY SENNA AND THE GAME OF FASCINATION...
THERE'S EVERYTHING NOBLE ABOUT IT.
YA'KNOW,.. FASCINATION AIN'T ALL THAT FUN BY YOURSELF, BUT –
SUIT YOURSELF!..

DINNNNNNNG!!
SINCE BEFORE YOU WERE BORN
THE BEAT
THE END
WELL, WELL, WELL...
WITH A LITTLE LUCK AND A
LOT OF DETERMINATION,
YOU WON!!..
AND ON THE
DIAGNAL LINE!..
CONGRATULATIONS!..
LET'S SEE YOU
DO IT AGAIN!..
Mr. Fascin

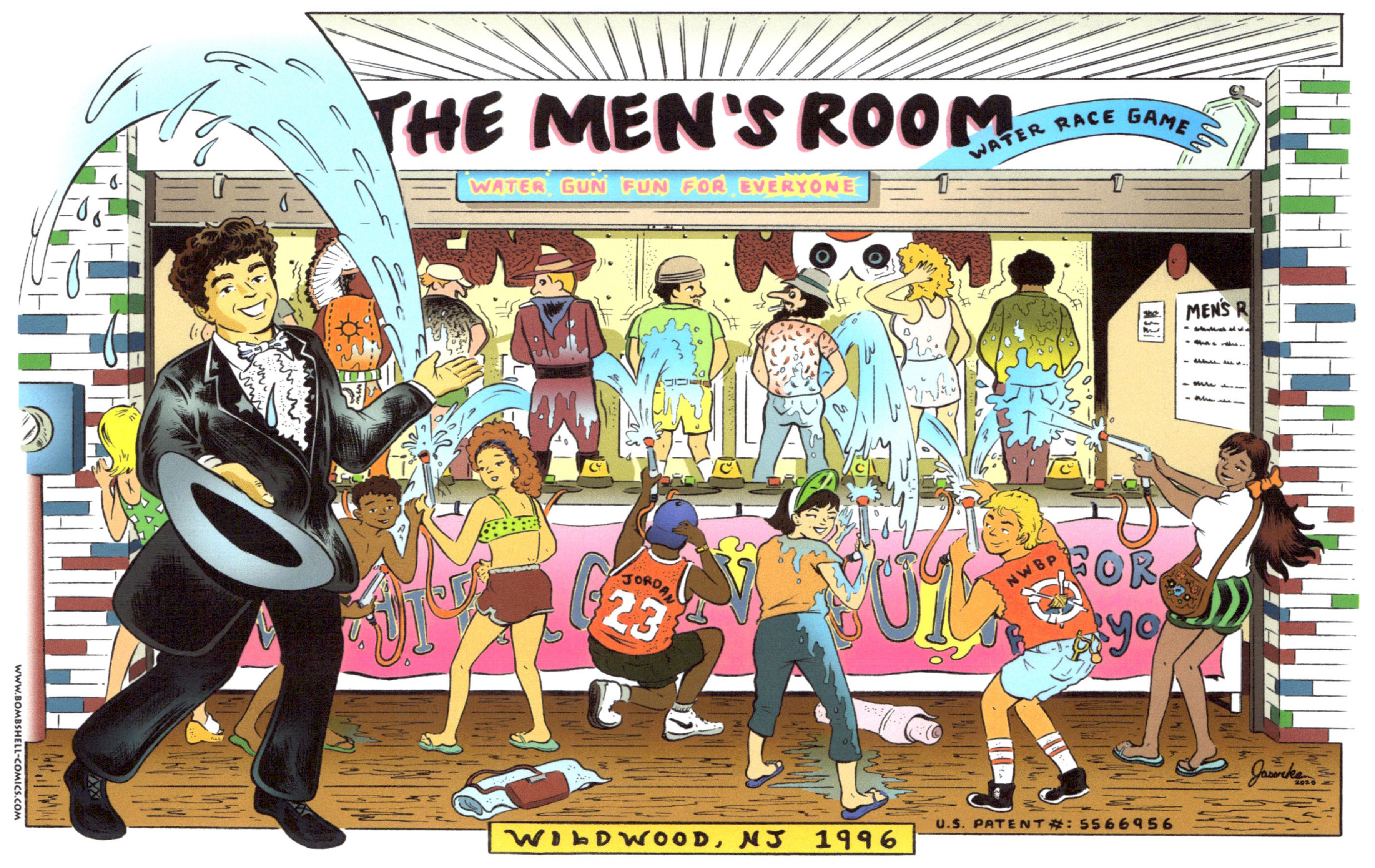

THE MEN'S ROOM
WATER RACE GAME
WATER GUN FUN FOR EVERYONE
MEN'S R
JORDAN 23
NWBP
FOR
yo
WILDWOOD, NJ 1996
U.S. PATENT #: 5566956
WWW.BOMBSHELL-COMICS.COM

THE KEEPER OF THE FLAME